Where Godly Men Walked

Life Journey From Here to Eternity

BY
Willie Johnson

This book is dedicated to countless aspiring men and women who have the call of God on their lives. It is designed to help prepare them for many of the challenges that lie ahead of them in ministry. My aim is to show from everyday life experiences, that without a progressing relationship with God, our goals, high hopes, and gifts mean nothing at all. In addition, this book will help give direction to men and women who have been in ministry as pastor, evangelist, or laity. Its purpose is to reveal the truth of God by application of His Word and to persuade sinners to be saved. As Christians, we will be reminded of our heritage, and challenge the sinner to repent. The readers will be motivated and inspired to give themselves more completely to God without reservation.

This book makes no claim to replace the regular study of your Bible. But it serves as a compass for the next generation to lead godly men and women in re-discovering the fundamental elements upon which godly lives are built. While the title of this book is *Where Godly Men Walked*, it also applies to godly women. In most instances, the use of the word *Men* means mankind, thus, referring to both men and women.

WILLIE JOHNSON

WHERE GODLY MEN WALKED

Life Journey From Here to Eternity
VOLUME III (NEW EDITION)

WILLIE JOHNSON

WHERE GODLY MEN WALKED

Life Journey From Here to Eternity
VOLUME III (NEW EDITION)

ARPress
ILLUMINATING IDEAS
EMPOWERING VOICES

ARPress
45 Dan Road Suite 15
Canton MA 02021
  Hotline: 1(888) 821-0229
  Fax: 1(508) 545-7580

Ordering Information:
Quantity sales. Special discounts are available on quantity purchases by corporations, associations, and others. For details, contact the publisher at the address above.

Printed in the United States of America.

ISBN-13:   Softcover   979-8-89676-459-5
            eBook   979-8-89676-460-1
            Hardback   979-8-89676-461-8

Library of Congress Control Number: 2025919452

Contents

Acknowledgments

I would like to thank my parents, John and Lucy Johnson. It is because of you that I was born into the world and have become the man that I am. The joining of your lives has made this book possible. What you taught me were the basics and foundational things needed to set me on my life's course. Thank you for your love and kindness.

Thanks to you Barbara, my loving wife. God gave me a gem when He gave you to me. Standing faithfully by my side, you have been a great support and encouragement to me. You are so special to me, and I love you.

Thanks to Lore and Veronica, my two daughters who always had faith in me no matter what the situation. I could not have hoped for a more precious two-some than you. Thanks for believing in me.

Next, I want to thank all others whom God has placed in my life through many years of ministry. Thanks to Adrienne Johnson for your beginning support; and to Idel Williams who was my teacher. Thanks to the pastors, leaders, and the rest who have helped to shape me as my Heavenly Father molded me into whom He wanted me to be.

I am grateful for many lessons well learned.

Above all: I thank my Lord and Savior Jesus Christ for making it all happen. Without Him nothing is possible. All the glory and honor I give to Him for His great salvation and for the privilege of sharing His Word.

Editor's Page

Contributing Editors

Editor one. . . . . Lisa Renée Clark

Thank you, Renee, for the time and energy you poured into the editing of this book. Your devotion and expertise have made a great impact on its outcome. May God bless you for all you have done in helping to make this book a success.

Editor two. . . . . .Lord Song Editing Division

Thank you, Lord Song, for the outstanding services you provided for this project, your assistance will never be forgotten.

Editor three. . . . . Barbara Johnson

I give a very special thanks to my lovely wife and partner in life, Barbara. Your added touch to the editing of this book brought it into clear perspective, and your contribution of time and effort brought it to the place of publication. I love you.

Introducing
Where Godly Men Walked

Out of the shadows of history they came as champions: men and women who were called by God and empowered to shape history. They were clad with the armor of faith, wielding the sword of the Spirit, which is the word of God, and on their vesture was written—Heroes of the faith.

And as champions by nature, the nature of God; they came bearing the light of Jesus Christ who is the eternal light of glory. By the Spirit of the Lord, these champions were ignited with the power to affect change for generations to come.

And because they succeeded in their mission, we can now boldly carry their message to a dying world declaring the Word of God today. The brightness of the word brought us light. This brilliant light of the word shines from eternity to eternity, and by it all of humanity can see the path *Where Godly Men Walked.*

Chapter 1

From Here to Eternity

Every person born into this world is born with a purpose and a destiny. There is a purpose for the lifetime that every man and woman will spend on earth as they interact with their fellow man. And when time and purpose are complete, they must give way to destiny.

God created time, purpose, and destiny not for Himself, but for mankind. Time and purpose center on the here and now, but destiny focuses on the hereafter. One's destiny actually begins with the condition of their soul at the end of life in this physical world. After this comes the eternal state.

Everyone comes into this physical world by birth, a process that cannot be reversed, and so it will be once we reach our destiny at the end of this life as we enter the eternal state. The transition will be irreversible.

These two things pertaining to life are certain. First, we must choose the way of life we are going to live. Secondly, we will be held accountable for the lifestyle we choose. We live within the boundaries of time, but we were designed for eternity.

Although time will come to an end one day, the fruit of one's labors in this life will be their reward for eternity. The condition of our souls at the point of death reflects largely on decisions we have made throughout our lifetime. Since our time on earth is limited, we must make a deliberate effort to seize this God-given opportunity to live lives that please Him, when we do; we are being prepared for eternity. God is in control of it all, so He has given the Church His Holy Spirit to orchestrate His affairs here on earth. He wants every man to learn His ways, and only then can we come to know our purpose in His divine plan.

Our purpose is realized within time, while the performance of it prepares us for eternity.

Time and Eternity

Time and eternity can relate to each other, because in one way they are similar to each other. What I mean is; the kind of life we choose to live here within time will leave lasting effects into eternity.

Time: Time reveals our habits, the kind of decisions we have made, and the lifestyle we have chosen to live. As adults the condition of our lives largely reflects on decisions we have made early on in life, so our choices shape our lives.

This is why it is crucial for people to come to know our heavenly Father at the earliest stages in life.

Proverbs chapter 22 and verse 6 commands parents *to "Train up a child in the way he should go, and when he is old he will not depart from it"*.

When we look back over our life and see that many years have passed; it is easy to think that time is so long. But compared to eternity, it is only for a moment, and the fruit of the lifestyle we kept here will follow us into eternity.

Eternity: The condition of the soul when facing eternity will reflect on decisions we made in time. Once we enter the eternal state, we cannot go back to make corrections. This is why we need the guidance of the Holy Spirit because He is the one who orders our steps according to God's word.

"But the Comforter, which is the Holy Ghost, whom the Father will send in my name, he shall teach you all things, and bring all things to your remembrance, whatsoever I have said unto you" John chapter 14 and verse 26 (KJV).

No man will have the option to come back and relive this physical life because the Bible says to us: *It is appointed unto men once to die, but after this the judgment Hebrews chapter 9 and verse 27 (KJV).*

Since it is appointed unto us once to die, we need to use every resource God has made available to us which teaches us His ways. Only then can we come to know our purpose in His divine plan. He is our wisdom and He knows what is best for each of us. It has been said that King Solomon, Israel's third king, was one of the wisest men ever to live, read *1 Kings chapter 10 and verses 6–7 and 23–24).* He ruled over Israel for forty years. Well, where did his wisdom come from? It came from God! You and I may not be called upon to be a king as in Solomon's case, or to possess the kind of wisdom it would take to rule a kingdom; but God desires to embrace our lives as He did the life of King Solomon. God's plan for his life is what brought him to greatness.

Prior to his call, Solomon would have remained just an ordinary figure in history without God. The scripture reminds us: *"For without me you can do nothing" (John chapter 15 and verse 5 (KJV).*

It is amazing that although the Lord does not need the help of any man to accomplish his purpose, through grace He invites us to co-operate with him in this process as He prepares us for our destiny with Him. God invests much into people who take time to seek His face until He responds. Solomon received God's wisdom and understanding by asking for it in prayer and making supplications to Him. God responded to him with an answer that even Solomon could not have imagined. *Read 1 Chronicles chapter 1 and verses 7–12* for more on this topic.

The Bible does not tell us if Solomon had an agenda of his own, or if he had any selfish ambitions at this time in his life. Being a newly appointed King, he realized his inadequacy to perform the duties of the office to which he had been called. The first and maybe the most important requirement was his willingness to be taught by God, so he bowed himself and humbly submitted to God, the one who knew him better than he knew himself. It was crucial for Solomon to get his instructions from God, because the life of the nation of Israel would be directly influenced by the words and actions of their new king.

The Power of Influence

Have you ever seriously asked yourself, *how does my life affect the lives of other people?* Maybe a few people have complimented you on certain positive qualities you possess, and you thought you were okay. What I mean is, they say something nice about you while they are in your presence, but when they leave you, do they have to re-evaluate you or question whether you are truly a Christian?

Now, of course, we cannot start living life to please everyone else, however we do need to live our lives as representatives of Christ because we all influence other people in one way or another.

As Christians, we must be able to influence the lives of others for good through practical, Christian living; not in piety, but as humble servants of God. We must be reachable and approachable servants sent by the Lord to represent Him. Now that is influence. So, while we live out our lives in the time that has been loaned to us by God, we please Him through our faithful service to those around us. While aiming high and heading for eternity; we simultaneously influence the lives of other people for good daily through our acts of love. Since time is one thing the human race will never have too much of, we must use it wisely so that the succeeding generations will realize God's Word is the rule and the standard by which we must live. God is passionately interested in generations.

He looks ahead and sees the next generations that are coming, and as with us; His compassionate heart and gentle hand will lead each one of them who is willing to follow Him. We are His workmanship, as stated in Ephesians chapter 2 and verse 10 (KJV).

It states: *"For we are His workmanship, created in Christ Jesus unto good works, which God hath before ordained that we should walk in them."*

By God's design, the shaping of His workmanship results in mature Christians who have conformed to the image of Jesus, His Son, giving them influence in the world.

Jesus fully understood the power of influence. He knows that the value system of one generation will affect succeeding generations for eternity. God has blessed each of us with the natural ability to influence the lives of other people, even when we are not aware of it. Throughout biblical history, we can find examples of the power of influence for evil and for good. The *Webster's Dictionary* definition of influence is, *"power exerted over the minds or behavior of others."*

Your influence on the lives of other people can motivate them to make decisions. Each day of your life you influence other people in one way or another. The power of influence works on the principle of faith. A degree of trust is involved. In the same way when we love someone, that trust makes itself vulnerable, even to the possibility of getting hurt. But if our love is truly genuine and sincere, we know that along with the possibility of getting hurt, there is equally an opportunity and the chance to spend a lifetime of good with our new loved one. It goes without saying that influence can be very rewarding when it results in something good.

Influence is powerful as its definition states.

Your influence has the power to either help or hinder the progress of other people. Our influence on others should always be for good and never for evil, so we should express humility in our daily lives as Jesus did. Humility must be the driving force behind every Christian's influence, and the world should be getting its cues from us.

Jesus was a man of humility, although some people mistook his humility for weakness. Humility actually demonstrates to us strength under control, and Jesus proved this in how He interacted with others. While helping some people, others ridiculed Him, but He did not allow this to affect His mission or His reason for coming into the world. His life has affected the whole world for good like no one else for all of time and eternity. So, in order for our lives to influence the world for good as Jesus' followers, we must exhibit the same humility expressed by our Lord. When people see us, they should see Him because we are His children.

People need our help, encouragement and love. Let's give it all right here and now while there is still time. There are no needs to be met in heaven, because then we will be in the presence of the all-sufficient One where there is no lack or need of anything.

Once there were two people having a conversation about this life and eternity. One man made this statement: I know that Heaven is up there, but "Heaven can wait." The point he was making was to say: Just let me live life with all the gusto I can right now. I'm not in heaven yet. Although that sounds like a cliché and somewhat presumptuous; I think there is something in it worth observing. This saying could well apply to anyone who claims they are on their way to heaven but they have not taken seriously their God-given responsibility here on earth to love their neighbors as themselves.

Our work here on earth will never be effective if we are so heavenly minded that we are not influencing others for good by sharing the love of God. We would do well to examine our hearts daily in the light of God's Holy Word. After all, it is here among people where we prepare for heaven, and it takes a lifetime to do that. Heaven will be ready for us when we arrive.

Persistence Against Opposition

During old and New Testament times, godly men and women set their sights on the future as eternity illuminates in their hearts. They never lost their God-given purpose and the sense of being responsible for the needs of people. Their goal was to please God. They continued to work toward that goal while keeping themselves pure and unspotted from the deceptions of Satan and the world. They continued until the God of glory completed His work in them. They were then perfectly fitted for eternity.

"To everything there is a season, and a time to every purpose under the heaven" Ecclesiastes chapter 3 and verse 1 (NKJV).

It is so easy to get sidetracked and deceived by counterfeits and to miss the times and seasons that God ordains for us in situations of life. There are times of joy and times of sorrow, times we can relax, and then there are those times when we are tested. God will at times allow testing to come to strengthen our faith. He never tempts us; only Satan does that. Satan, the enemy and adversary of God; seeks to deceive the people of God. He seeks to destroy our influence. Satan often makes us feel like no one else is going through what we are going through. But the truth is; everyone is facing some kind of adversity, temptation, trial, setback, delay, or discouragement. Out of the list above, temptation is at the top of Satan's list. If he is successful in getting us to yield to his temptations, we enable him to use the rest of the list against us. Satan is the father of lies and deception. The attacks he make are used like tools designed to get us to focus all our attention on ourselves and to become so pre-occupied with what is happening to us that we're not helping others who have a need. It is that form of the "me, me and only me" pride that caused him to be cast out of the same heaven that God has prepared for you and me to enjoy. History holds the record that godly men chose right when they accepted God's plan for their lives over what Satan had planned for them.

"And truly, if they had been mindful of that country from whence they came out, they might have had opportunity to have returned. But now they desire a better country, that is, a heavenly; wherefore God is not ashamed to be called their God; for he hath prepared for them a city" Hebrews chapter 11 and verses 15-16 (KJV).

Life is not always fair, and we will certainly suffer some of that unfairness. But we don't give up when it happens. We get over it and continue on our journey of influencing others for the Master. His plan for us is not only about where we are, but it is ultimately about where we are going, because our future is secure in Christ.

Think of an insurance policy. We pay into it in case of an accident or some future misfortune. In the event that something happens, we are covered. Unlike insurance, which we may never need; the assurance God provides is needed for this journey and its benefits are far greater.

The rewards we receive for our life service to Him here on earth cover us for all eternity.

On this journey of Godly men, we will uncover the secrets to their strength and dedication to God. They determined within themselves that there would be no limits on their venture. They were willing to walk out by faith and explore uncharted territory, and places where the status quo and mediocre kind of Christian only talked about going. For Godly men and women, the stakes are never too high. They will take a chance on Jesus by using their faith when others say it is too risky. Now according to natural reasoning, it may very well be risky, but Godly men will take a chance on Jesus; knowing that their steps are ordered by the Lord. As you step out in obedience to God with a trusting heart, Jesus makes every step you take a sure one.

"He will not suffer thy foot to be moved, He that keeps thee will not slumber" *Psalm chapter 121 and verse 3 (KJV).*

Faith says, when we cannot see God's hand, we learn to trust His heart. There will always be times of testing for godly men and women in life.

The test is always designed to align us with God's best for our lives, and that's enough for us to take courage and to use our faith.

Only godly men have learned the priceless value of patiently waiting for the Lord to act while making themselves content in the waiting.

"For I have learned in whatever state I am, to be content" *Philippians chapter 4 and verse 11 (KJV).*

When we learn to patiently wait on the Lord and be content while being tested, we will come to recognize God's divine timing and seasons for our lives. Contentment is a component of patience. Patience is a virtue that each of us must learn to exercise while God is at work in our lives. Our days, weeks, months and years are all written in His book of life, and He moves us from one step to the next in His awesome plan.

Every now and then on this Christian journey, we come into unexpected curves on the road, at other times we end up at a roadblock. These experiences are the times when we can't see clearly what the Lord is doing behind the scenes and frustration sets in. During these times, we must learn to be prayerful and careful to ask God for discernment, because the setting may be a time or place when God is at work forming and reforming our character. Before we know it, we could respond bitterly to the adversity, forgetting that sometimes God may allow difficulty or some kind of trouble to come in the process of drawing us closer to Him. It is easy to view our troubles as an attack from the enemy. For this, daily prayer is so important, because in prayer we get the answers we need. Our dilemma or adversity may not necessarily be a trap that was set by the enemy. If we will stop and examine it carefully, we may see the handprints of the Savior on it.

The whole reason behind your present trial may not yet be realized. Whatever the reason, God works *all things together for good to those who love the Lord* according to *Romans chapter 8 and verse 28*. God will show us the proper responses in such situations to help us not to react on an impulse, which would leave us open to attacks from the enemy. The right response silences the enemy, and builds our confidence.

Confidence in the Savior

God's way for us is not complicated. He makes it plain for us.

"He has shown you oh man, what is good, and what the lord requires of you, but to do justly, and to love mercy, and to walk humbly with your God" Micah chapter 6 and verse 8 (NKJV).

We must learn to open our eyes to all that the Lord is revealing to His body and to understand His ways.

Proverbs Chapter 4 and verse 7 says to us: "Wisdom is the principal thing; so get wisdom: and with all your getting, get understanding."

Discernment is a gift from God. Without it, it is easy to confuse what seems to be a negative situation with something that God is really in control of. So be suspicious of that bend in the road up ahead; and yes, even that roadblock may have been orchestrated by the Lord; for divine purposes not yet revealed.

"For my thoughts are not your thoughts, neither are your ways my ways says the Lord" Isaiah chapter 55 and verse 8 (KJV).

God's thoughts are higher than the thoughts of mankind; neither can one figure out the mind of the Lord, because His ways are past finding out.

But we can rest assured that He always knows and does what is best for His people, and that He will not leave us in the dark about what He does.

In *Revelation chapter 1 and verse 1,* the first five words are *"The Revelation of Jesus Christ".* The word "revelation" means to take the cover off.

The Greek form of the word is *apokalupsis*. It means the unveiling of the glory of Christ. It also signifies that this glory would not have been known if God had not chosen to reveal it.

"Eye hath not seen, nor ear heard, neither have entered into the heart of man, the things which God hath prepared for them that love Him" 2 Corinthians chapter 2 and verse 9 (KJV).

We love Him but He loves us more than we could ever imagine. He wants His children to know His will for their lives. God wants us to look to Him as our ultimate source of direction. The Holy Spirit is an influencer. We are informed and enabled by Him. We can get plenty of information from a culture that is flooded with it. However, if that information is incorrect or unreliable, it is information that is good for nothing. The most important thing is to be led by the Holy Spirit who *"teaches us all things, and brings all thing back to our remembrance" John chapter 16 and verses 13-15 (KJV).*

The way to know if what we are doing will be right and profitable for the work of God is to examine it through revelation of the scriptures. If we keep doing something and it is not working, we need to keep seeking God in prayer because He promised to hear us when we pray and seek Him with all our heart according to Hebrews chapter 5 and verse 7 (KJV). God directs and corrects us as we humble ourselves, seek His face, and turn from our own ways according to *2 Chronicles chapter 7 and verse 14 (NKJV).*

The Christian life is often compared to a relay race. The baton is passed to those who will carry it on. Jesus, being our forerunner, expects us to pick up where He left off, to step in stride, and to keep the momentum. We must lay hold of the baton and carry it on to the finish line. As we do, others will realize God's power to equip everyone who receives the Lord Jesus Christ. We cannot afford to miss such a golden opportunity for Him.

The anointing that God has poured out on this generation is absolutely awesome. It raises the most unlikely among men and women to walk in places of service with a boldness never known before.

There is a call of the Spirit in these days, as God positions us to meet the mandate He has set for the end times. There is a shifting in the spirit realm. It comes to align the body of Christ, and to equip us for this hour. This is the hour for significant breakthroughs in healing, finances, and to prosper in the work of the ministry. This breakthrough includes a transfer of the hoarded wealth of the world into the church for the purpose of spreading the gospel to the ends of the world. Get ready! God has prepared this generation for the great end-time harvest. This could well be the finest hour of the church in our time. I pray that we will realize it and not miss our season as the Jewish people did in

Jesus' day *(Luke 13:34-35)*. For this reason, we need to respond to the Holy Spirit's call with a resounding, "Lord, shake us again!"

Chapter 2

Mindsets, Methods, and Concepts

Mindsets

In the 1980s and 90s in my first years of being a Pastor; I learned many valuable lessons about God, people, and life. Many lessons were easy, but some I learned in the school of hard knocks. Many difficult situations taught me to seek the face of God.

The bible says *"Let this mind be in you which was also in Christ Jesus: who being in the form of God, thought it not robbery to be equal with God: but made himself no reputation, and took upon himself the form of a servant, and was made in the likeness of men" Philippians chapter 2 and verse 5 (KJV).*

Everyone, even the sinner, knows that there is a higher power, someone greater than we are. No one can ignore the evidence that creation presents. There is an eternal God who lives and abides forever. Yet He chose to do something totally against all that the world believes about God. God, who is eternal, said, "I (Jesus) will die and redeem them." *Verse 8 of Philippians chapter 2* says *"He humbled himself and became obedient unto death, even the death of the cross."*

The question then arises, how can the God who lives and abides forever say, "I will die"? My prayer is that by the end of this chapter you will be able to answer that question. But for now, I want to draw you to The Power of a Mindset.

We will never become gods as some religions of the world teach. But we are made in the image of God and possess certain characteristics and abilities given to us through His eternal power. One thing that has been very damaging to the body of Christ and the world has to do with "particular mindsets".

As a young pastor, I had my own preconceived ideas about who God was, and how He was supposed to work in the lives of men and women.

As a child growing up, I was taught some things about the church and the Christian life. But later on in life a personal experience with the Lord showed me how I had allowed myself to be lured into a one-way mindset (according to the flesh, not according to God). Being ignorant concerning some things, I was limited and not sensitive to the Spirit of the Lord. Job said: *"He is in one mind and who can turn him" Job chapter 23 and verse 13 (KJV).*

Yes, God is in one mind. But that doesn't mean He has only one way to get the job done. We have the greatest of need to immerse ourselves in the Word of God until we get God's revelation of who He is, because we shut doors to blessings and smother opportunities for Christ with mindset limitations. So we broaden our horizons by listening to the voice of the Holy Spirit. Let God expand your thinking, remembering, that you grow only by what you know.

It is an awesome privilege when one is called to be a pastor. Yet it is a very serious assignment that should not be entered into lightly apart from the leading of the Holy Spirit. People sometimes start idolizing leaders, which is never a good thing. Often the pastor is stereotyped as one who has all the answers and the one who is to give the final word on a thing. Although we must be thankful for pastors and give them the honor due to them, we can never idolize them, when we do, we in effect are giving God a second-row seat to men. This must never be. What is your mindset, how do you view Pastors? Most people love Pastors and leaders with strong leadership qualities and abilities. However, church history has proven to us that too many people have depended on the pastor for too many things for too long. And perhaps they are this way because of a particular mindset they developed somewhere along the way. This mindset honors pastors through false humility and loads them down with responsibilities they were never meant to carry. Although pastors are gifts from God, they are not perfect. *"Let all things be done decently and in order" 1 Corinthians chapter 14 and verse 40 (KJV).* The church is made up of people – people who are not perfect.

Whenever problems arise in the local assembly, it is easy for a pastor or leader who has just begun in the ministry to handle some situations wrong because of a lack of experience. For this reason, this man or woman of God needs to have those to whom they can be accountable; those whom they can pray with, yet people who can be objective and give them constructive criticism.

Pastors cannot afford to be led by their feelings. They must beware of assuming that it is their responsibility to straighten out the members, or to put people in their place with God's word.

"Humble yourselves therefore under the mighty hand of God, that He may exalt you in due time" James chapter 5 and verse 6 (KJV).

When God calls one into a leadership position, it is not because he or she has arrived. Usually there are at least two factors involved with the call. First factor: He teaches you as the leader. Second factor: He reaches others through you. The leader must simply hear it, exemplify it, and pass it on. Then everyone is blessed and God is glorified.

Methods

In order for any corporation, church, or individual to be successful in what they do, they need a strategy, and that with wise counsel.

"Where there is no counsel, the people fall: but in the multitude of counselors there is safety" Proverbs chapter 11 and verse 14 (NKJV).

It is no secret that everyone has a different method or way of doing things. People probably use as many methods of doing things; as there are stars in the heavens. I believe God loves variety. I also believe that God loves it even when we apply different methods as we accomplish the work of the kingdom. We run into trouble when the method becomes entirely the means to accomplishment. Churches have split and even entire organizations have been dissolved because of an argument over a method. Yes, we must learn to use every resource God has made available to us for the work of His kingdom. And we all are free to choose our own method, but we must remember never to let our method become the law by which we are to determine everything. God will bless the method we may use only if it agrees with His divine plan. As we yield to Him in obedience, the Holy Spirit shows us what pleases Him as He orchestrates the affairs of His church.

"And there are diversities of operations, but the same God which works all in all" 1 Corinthians chapter 12 and verse 6 (KJV).

Diversities in the Greek language is: "Diairesis". It means that the Spirit bestows certain gifts to certain people. In order for our gifts to be truly effective, they must be used for the building of God's kingdom on earth. Whatever the method, it should always be founded upon the principles of God's word. Only then will we have His approval.

A vision for a successful Pastor must be paramount. When the Lord gives one, usually the Pastor can see it ahead of them as complete. But the caution I would give them is this: People, yes, even lovable God-fearing people who honor you as their leader will not always be able to see the full scope of your vision as you do. Even your method may at times seem foreign to them. Some people will need time to grasp it. Time will allow it to grow on them. So a Pastor must let patience be built into the foundation of what they do. The pastor or leader who would please God is flexible and his life pliable. This does not suggest that he or she is a weakling, but it means that the application of these traits contributes to the health of the church body.

A pastor or leader must also be open to the working of the Holy Spirit to be alert to what is happening in the lives of the flock they have been called to shepherd. There may be times when he will have to address anyone who holds a position of leadership in the church; who has allowed their pride to create strife among the flock. They cannot afford to allow this; it would be a stumbling block or a hindrance to the momentum of the work and growth of others in the church. Looking out for the flock is at the top of the list of their duties.

There is no greater tragedy than for a pastor or any leader to be blind to the growth and maturity of those they have instructed. And they must not be fearful, or jealous; nor feel threatened by the ones who have matured under their leadership. Things like this open doors for contentions and strife among the body of believers. Growing to new levels of maturity is the goal, and everyone has a capacity to serve, and gifts to offer.

God has provided spiritual gifts to edify the body within the local assembly and beyond its four walls. Everyone has a gift, and not everyone is called to be a pastor or teacher within the church. Some people within the body are called to evangelize, or to be a prophet, or maybe as a singer who travels and ministers the word of God.

Pastors must allow the Lord to settle, and to mature them on this their God-given platform. In doing so they can seize the opportunity to make their calling and election sure (Read II Peter chapter 1 and verses 10-11). In this process, God is bringing you as a leader; to a level of maturity while simultaneously bringing the congregation also to a level of maturity. As God instructs the leader as to what He wants, the people can receive God's instructions and grow in their walk with Him.

Those who were effective pastors and leaders in Biblical times were the ones who had vision. As they made themselves available to the Lord, He listened and responded to them. God moved them to choose methods that would affect positive change in their world. In order for people's lives to be changed and to be productive for the work of the Lord, there is the necessity to be inspired by the Holy Spirit.

But when people try to implement their ideas of how the work of the kingdom should be done, they begin to use scheme-based methods that are usually non-productive. This can lead people to fall into error, thus; hindering the flow of the Holy Spirit and this becomes a snare to Christian growth.

Biblical history of the Church has shown to us that when it is not willing to move with the flow of the Spirit of God as He wishes, He has been known to force change upon it. For more information on this subject, read Revelation chapter 2 and verse 16.

One night in a dream the Lord showed me a church that had refused to repent or to reform. His view of it was as an adulterous woman. She was what the Bible calls; "estranged" which means having turned to another; from Him. She (the church) had lost her first love, and her mind was not on Him any more, only on other things. But God was waiting with a heart of such intense love that it was indescribable. The one and only thing that could release the flood of His compassion towards her was repentance. Repentance releases the flood of God's compassion; which brings godly success in ministry. To successfully walk out our faith, we need to get the mind of Christ. So, whenever we choose a method, the wise thing to do is to let it be bathed in prayer to God before applying it.

It is necessary to remember that whatever our method of doing things even with the purest of motives and intentions; we must know that God is the one who makes the final judgment on it. For that reason, the man or woman of God must remain open to the Holy Spirit for knowledge and revelation from God.

Concepts

To embark upon a venture in life without first having a concept of how to go about it is a guaranteed failure. A concept is the plant that comes from the seed of a mindset.

The way we see ourselves will affect how far we go in life. Also, our words will aid in either advancing us or setting us back. Because our words affect our lives more than we think, we must be careful not to speak against our own hope. It is true that God expects us to set goals in life and to make plans for the future, which is an act of faith. But remember that we can't put together something that is not according to what God has planned.

God's Word says: *"A man's heart devises His way: but the Lord directs his steps" Proverbs chapter 16 and verse 9 (KJV).*

There have been times in my life that I had my eyes set on certain goals and thought I had God's approval, only to be disappointed because I followed my own concept and not His will on how to reach them. Since the mind-set was not right my concept of what His will was for my life was wrong.

When we persistently attempt to lead ourselves, we are asking for trouble. This is where we give the enemy an open door into this life journey. Satan speaks to us and even our own flesh suggests to us some things to do. There are many persuasive voices speaking spiritual things, so don't be deceived, we need to be sure of who is speaking to us. When we know this, we can expect growth, because the Christian life is about growing in Christ. Be aware that the Lord is always looking to bring us to higher levels of maturity in Him. We need to make our calling and election sure. By prayers and seeking the Lord you will know who is speaking to you, and you won't go wrong. Whatever our area of Ministry, when we do that with all our heart, we won't be led away into some area of ministry that we have not been called to. Beware of the people that sometimes may see your God-given gifts, and His anointing on your life, who attempt to prostitute these gifts for their own desire. There are those who even try to pressure you to go into some Ministry that perhaps you have not been called to. They want to tell you what Ministry God has called you to. I have found that this is a concept that should be avoided.

Of course there aren't any Lone Ranger (stand alone) Christians in the work of the Lord, we will always need the support of others in the work of Christ. But as we commit ourselves to service in God's house, we should remain aware of the calling with which we have been called. We must be aware of false concepts of service for God, and at the same time, be open to receive the help of other people as God fulfills His plan in our lives. If God has commissioned you for a specific work for Him, others should serve only to confirm God's call on your life, rather than to affirm it.

Many people have not lived their lives to their greatest potential because too often they wait for other people's affirmation of them. It is always wise for us to listen to the advice of those whom God puts among us to reassure us of things He has said to us or done. However, He expects us to be sure within our own heart as He deals with us directly. This is where relationship with the Lord is born (*read 2 Peter chapter 1 and verse 10*). Personally, I believe that there needs to be times in your Christian life when it is just you and your Lord spending that special quality time together, those times when you can hear a word from God for yourself; He longs for these times.

Second Timothy chapter 2 and verse 15 says: *"Study to show thyself approved unto God, a workman that need not to be ashamed, rightly dividing the word of truth." (KJV).*

God longs for us to spend quality time with Him studying His Word, meditating on it, and praying to Him. Those are the times when we get our clearest instructions from Him, and when we can be as intimate with Him as much as He wants to be with us. One reason why the word we preach so often fails to affect change in the lives of those who hear us; is because of the tragedy of not spending sufficient time in God's presence to get His concept of things. After all, the only way that we can lay *"precept upon precept; and line upon line" (Isaiah 28:10)* is to get God's concept of things. The result is to have His mind according to *Philippians chapter 2 and verse 5 (KJV).*

The word of God must be the most important thing in our lives. We need to pray to enter into the knowledge of His perfect will for us. God expects us to seek Him and daily resort to Him until we have developed a progressive relationship with Him.

This new generation has suffered a great loss of spiritual and moral fervor because of the change in value systems. This generation has a different concept of what Christianity really is. The Bible says, *"Where your treasure is there will your heart be also," (Matthew chapter 6 and verse 21).*

The most recent generations don't seem to know the basics and the fundamentals upon which our lives are to rest. You don't hear words in their conversations like: Wholesome, Sanctification, and Integrity. Godly men and women will teach their children Biblical values in order to preserve coming generations. We as a people need to return to these values, because they define a society, and they say to the world who, and whose we are. Godly values are the building blocks for a healthy society that will last a thousand years. All this will come from spending time in the presence of the Lord.

People usually spend most of their time around whatever or whomever they love most. They have put certain values on them. In an age of quick fixes, microwaves, and the so-called sexual revolution; having the world at our fingertips, it's easy to be distracted from what matters most and lose sight of wholesome values and godly standards. But godly men of old did not allow themselves to be distracted with the pace of society nor the standards of the world. They had their sights set for the long haul, and their hopes in the one who holds eternity; God Himself.

Yield your mind to Christ, and He will enable you to guard your heart against the distractions of the times. Although God is not bound by time, He has obligated Himself to operate within the boundaries of time as He governs the lives of men.

"Heaven and earth shall pass away, but my word shall stand forever" *Matthew chapter 24 and verse 35 (KJV).*

Men and women who walk with God should be continually progressing, and never regressing. This does not mean that they won't have some setbacks. But when God is involved, even setbacks become setups so that He can take us to the next level of maturity in Christ Jesus.

"And we know that all things work together for good to them who love God, to them who are called according to his purpose" *Romans chapter 8 and verse 28 (KJV).*

I have seen this scripture fulfilled in my life in unexpected ways. We often apply this scripture to adversity or negative things. But the way the Lord may choose to work that good in your life may be unconventional. My experience was this: In order to get me to the next level of maturity, at one point He began placing me among thinkers; people who had higher levels of thinking and with greater expectations; entrepreneurs, and business people who were goal oriented to expand my thinking.

Concepts come from mindsets. If we spend time around great thinkers or people with higher levels of thinking in society, we will eventually begin to think and act like they do in many ways. A person who has mastered some great tasks is able to build our confidence in that area so we can see our need to change our concept of some things. Sometimes we just need to change our way of thinking.

Ultimately God wants to build His character within us. So, He stretches our faith by drawing us through grace into new concepts. For a Christian, healthy concepts come from having the mind of Christ.

"Let this mind be in you, which was also in Christ Jesus" Philippians chapter 2 and verse 5 (KJV).

King David was an example of one having a right concept of things. God would exalt him to greatness in the eyes of His people Israel, but not without building the man's character in him first. David could not have been as the scripture declares: *"a man after God's own heart"* without this process. Before one can possess the character of God, they must have a proper concept of who He is. When this happens; any hindrances that may arise won't be able to stop their progress.

David is the writer of most of the Psalms in the Bible. In many of his writings, we find some of the most encouraging words in scripture. If you will be honest, we will agree that much of what David wrote then fits many of our personal life situations today. He talks from his experiences. He had a life of continual dependence upon God to empower him with the ability to get the victory in so many areas of his life. We see victory after victory from the time he kept his father's sheep until he became the king of Israel; and on throughout his lifetime.

Out of all that we read about David in the scriptures, no words reveal more clearly the reason for his continued success than the words *of Psalm 23.* There could have been no victories in his life apart from a personal relationship with God; which means he applied right concepts in his life as he served Jehovah. Often we are defeated, anxious, and frustrated in areas of our lives because of unanswered prayers. Many times this is simply because we fail to maintain a personal relationship with the Lord to keep us on course.

It is crucial that we seek to do God's will daily through prayer and the reading of His word. Then, as David, we can expect to have total victory in every area of our lives. Notice what David says in Psalm 23:4. *"Yea though I walk through the valley of the shadow of death, I will fear no evil: for you are with me: your rod and your staff, they comfort me."*

David had the assurance of God's ability to protect him in this situation because he had trusted Him in many others. David had fought many battles, but it was God who helped him win his many victories.

Victory comes only after a battle. God has designed it so that after the battle, we become more like the Savior. We are shaped into His image through adversity. As God provides a path through the place of adversity, we are encouraged to quietly and confidently wait for Him.

Just as Jesus on His way to Calvary would not be detoured from His course; but He would fulfill His mission, we also must be determined to trust and pass the test as God strengthens us through times of adversity. Notice that David said "... *I walk through the valley of the shadow of death*"... Don't make the mistake of stopping in the valley, but allow the Lord to carry you through it. Remember, we can't get beyond the valley without going through it. It is by God's design that our trials, tests, and the adversities of the Christian life come to last only for a season. So don't let your afflictions be a waste of time. Throw out the idea that God is out to get you because you are going through so many things in life. Learn to get His mind and know His heart for you. Revelation comes when you can see your life through His eyes. That's when you know you have the right concept of life.

Chapter 3

Suddenly Interrupted

The Checkpoint of Your Faith

To respond in obedience to God's call is no doubt the single most important responsibility that is given to men. God is holy, and the men and women who have realized this are the ones who have given themselves completely to Him without reservation. It is time for the people of God to realize that God is who He says He is, and He does not need to explain Himself in detail at every turn. As always, He requires that we learn to take Him at His word. Sometimes God is quick to answer a prayer or to solve a problem we might have, and at other times we may not be able to see His hand working things out so quickly. There may be a time when He doesn't cause the storm winds in our life to cease. Real faith comes to the surface at those times when we no longer have control of the situation.

What do you do when you know you have His word on a matter; you have received His instructions and you have begun to follow through on them, and then out of the blue you are suddenly interrupted and you come to realize that it was God who engineered it? You know this was an open door that you thought you were ready to step through, and suddenly there was a change of plans.

In the Bible, the eleventh chapter of Hebrews shares with us testimonies of men and women of God who are referred to as the Heroes of the faith. Well, did you know; that before they became heroes of this faith, they first of all were taken through a process that brought them to the checkpoint of their faith?

"After these things the word of the Lord came to Abram in a vision, saying, "Do not be afraid, Abram. I am your shield, and your exceedingly great reward." But Abram said, "Lord God, what will you give me, seeing I go childless, and the heir of my house is Eliezer of Damascus?" Then Abram said, "Look, you have given me no offspring; and indeed one born in my house is my heir." And behold, the word of the Lord came to him, saying, "This one shall not be your heir, but one who will come from your own body shall be your heir" Genesis chapter 15 and verses 1-4 (NKJV). Abram had God's promise, but he didn't fully know how God had planned to fulfill it, we see this in the next chapter where it says:

"Now Sarai, Abram's wife, had borne him no children. And she had an Egyptian maidservant whose name was Hagar. So Sarai said to Abram, See now, the Lord has restrained me from bearing children. Please, go into my maid; perhaps I shall obtain children by her." Notice the next sentence. *"And Abram heeded the voice of Sarai"* (chapter 16:1-4). As always, after God has made a promise to anyone, He then begins a process; bringing them to the checkpoint of their faith. The checkpoint is the place where their faith must be tested concerning the promise that has been given. In Genesis chapter 16 and verse 3 it appears that it was approximately ten years later since Abram had received the promise of his son Isaac; that Sarai offered her maidservant to him.

The passing of time will reveal to us the length of our patience and whether we believe the Lord for His promises.

An unknown author said it like this: "patience is the weapon that forces deception to reveal itself". Abram and Sarai had not expected such a span of time to elapse before Isaac would be born. This was the checkpoint of their faith. We know the story of God's promise of a son to Abram whose name would be Isaac which means laughter. Isaac would be a treasure in their possession because of the joy he would bring to them. But God would later ask Abram to sacrifice Isaac the son he loved so dearly.

You and I may at times have an Isaac in our lives, you know; those things we give lots of attention to. That thing we love the most. There are so many Isaacs in the lives of believers today. God put Abram's faith to the test and didn't really take Isaac's life.

Now, what is your Isaac? Whatever it is, remember that God tests each person's faith in a different way. To develop your faith, He may even kill your Isaac. Now naturally I don't mean the taking a life. But what I'm talking about is; if you are giving God second place to anything else in your life. God is not in the business of destroying life but giving it, yet He will not be counted second to any.

Because of God's call on Abram and Sarai's lives they needed unshakable faith; because they were being groomed and prepared for greatness. When God brings us to the checkpoint of our faith, He is calling us to greatness, a place of greater service, so He provides greater grace.

We prepare for the journey by relinquishing control and giving it to God. So put away any preconceived ideas or notions of how you think the promise he has made to you will come. The promises of God usually come with promotions attached to them. With each trial of life our faith is meant to grow. Using our faith is considered greatness in the eyes of God. Everyone whom the Lord has brought to greatness started out with simple child-like faith. On this faith journey you will always be faced with the pit stops of *"there's an easier way to accomplish this"*, or, there will always be the roadside rest stop of *"God doesn't mean for me to suffer such unfairness."*

Remember this: God always prepares the man or woman who is destined for greatness by refining them through trials and testing.

Although Abram and Sarai's actions had temporarily hindered the progress of what God had planned for them, God would shut down their plans by allowing them to see the futility of taking matters into their own hands. The plan could only work God's way. It would not be done merely because of consent on Abram's part alone. This was a Covenant between God who is perfect and Abram who was not.

Abram had not initiated the terms of this covenant. It was of Divine origin. This was a promise given by one who has never broken one. The promise had been confirmed by the introduction of the covenant. A covenant is a pact or agreement between two or more parties. This covenant was ratified by blood. Although at times God may shut doors that we have opened, many of which would delay his promise as in the case of Abram and Sarai; God is relentless in His pursuit in bringing it to pass through the process of a life of faith. His richest blessings come to us because of our covenant relationship with Him, but not without trials and testing. Sometimes before the promises of God come to the believer, He is silent. No doubt Abram experienced the same thing. When it seems that God is taking too long, we become impatient and we try to work it out ourselves. The results can be delayed fulfillment as in the matter of Hagar and Ishmael. Our attempts to help God out can only end in frustration and failure. As we learn to trust the Lord, He takes the helm to keep us on course.

Who's in Charge of Closed Doors?

God will always take the lead in the lives of them who are willing to trust Him no matter what. He wants us to learn to rest in Him and live with this confidence; that He will faithfully guide our footsteps and get us to the place where He wants us to be. When things don't work out for us, and doors don't open as we would like for them to; we have a tendency to become discouraged. But many valuable lessons can be learned in waiting, and we can achieve great things when doors are closed.

God is still in control even when He doesn't explain why He has not given you the answer to that prayer you have been praying. As a test of your faith, He may shut a door right in the middle of your plans so He can open a better one to fulfill His promise to you.

We tend to glide along when we see no great challenges to our faith. During such times, it gets easy to become relaxed or complacent.

We feel self-confident with our accomplishments. However, when we have challenges, God is at work on strengthening our faith. These are the times when God may choose to slow down the progression of a project we have embarked upon in order to change the direction in which we are headed. Whatever the situation, the outcome will ultimately be for our good and bring glory to God. God has many ways to work His will in us; many ways that are beyond our comprehension yet He enables us to succeed at it.

He has often chosen people who appear to be the most unlikely to succeed to use as instruments for opening new doors for others.

Look at the example of David who stood before King Saul in 1 Samuel chapter 18 and verses 2-8. Verse 2 says: "Saul took David that day, and would not let him go home to his father's house anymore."

Certainly, David had no plans of his own, nor did he have a grand scheme of becoming king prior to his election by God. He seemed to be satisfied with the humble occupation of keeping his father's sheep. No doubt he had a daily routine of caring for them and strategies on how to protect them from predators. But God had other plans for David and gave him favor with King Saul.

"...So David went out wherever Saul sent him, and behaved himself wisely..." 1 Samuel chapter 18 and verse 5.

We should always be aware that not everyone is happy for us when we're blessed.

"...So the women sang as they danced and said; Saul has slain his thousands, and David his ten thousands. Then, Saul was very angry, and the saying displeased him; and he said, they have ascribed to David ten thousands, and to me they have ascribed only thousands.....What more can he have but the kingdom?"

To respond in this way regarding someone who has been an asset to you or, to say the least; someone whose actions have made you look good says a lot about King Saul's character and his relationship. Because of insecurity and dishonesty, King Saul's heart was not right before God. This opened the door for the spirit of jealousy towards David. Saul also knew that God had chosen David to be the next king in Israel, this is what made him jealous. Jealousy has destroyed many friendships, even in the body of Christ. Although David would end up having to run for his life, God would use this unfortunate situation as an opportunity to raise a king who would be a man after His own heart.

For David, the expectation of continuing to serve with the king's favor toward him would turn out to be like a door slammed shut in his face. Although David would have to suffer for a while, the story does not end on a sad note for him. God would surely bless His servant. God was still in control in spite of Saul's continued attempts to close this open door, and He was working to open a greater one for David. Once opened, this door would remain open for the rest of his life and throughout the lives of his descendants. Ultimately through David's lineage would come the door by which the flock of God would enter into His (God's) rest. Jesus said: *"I am the door. If anyone enters by me, he will be saved, and will go in and out and find pasture" John chapter 10 and verse 9 (KJV).*

Joseph Jacob's son is another man who was blessed by God (Read *Genesis Chapter 41 and verses 37-43). He had some closed* doors as challenges to his faith. Being born into Abraham's lineage, he was an heir of the same promise. He was his father's favorite of all his sons. He would be blessed greatly by God, but envied greatly by his brothers who would deceive him and attempt to take his life. Anywhere there is deception and manipulation among people, there will always be hurt and disappointment. And so it was for Joseph and his family. Certainly, God's hand was on Joseph's life. This was clearly seen by the dreams God gave him. But sharing them with his brothers proved to be life threatening for him.

"And Joseph dreamed a dream, and he told it to his brethren, and they hated him yet the more" (Genesis 37:5).

God-given dreams will always be challenged by adversity, which will always be a part of life. My experience has been that it is not wise to reveal your dreams and visions to everyone because they can be delayed or even side tracked by people who are against you. It is best to pray for God's guidance and timing concerning them.

Joseph was a very happy young man having God's favor on his life. As long as Joseph thought his family would share his happiness, he continued to share his dreams with them. It is one thing to know that what you are sharing with your friends is being rejected, but to be rejected by your own family can be devastating. For Joseph, this was like a slap in the face, a show of disregard, or as a door slammed shut! However, God has a way of using unfortunate situations in our lives to bring glory to His name. With God, no trial, heartache, or disappointment is wasted. He takes them all into account and rewards the faithful.

Read an account of God's faithfulness in Romans Chapter 8:35-37.

God often brings our dreams and visions to their realization through adversity. If you trust God for the gifts He has put within you, you can never be silenced. The more people try to keep it from coming forth, the more God will magnify it in your life until there is no doubt that it is of God and not of men. God had a plan and a purpose for Joseph's life. He also has a plan and a purpose for your life, and whatever He starts He finishes. God is faithful to keep His promises to His people. So keep on standing strong in the service of the Lord. Keep moving forward toward your dream. When Satan attempts to get you to abort it, do not retreat. Learn to walk through the adversity trusting the Lord. Remember, He is faithful and you will not be disappointed! Never ever give up! It is always too soon to quit. In the midst of adversity is where

God builds His character within us. His purpose is to bless us and to make us a blessing to others.

Joseph was even thrown into a pit, sold into slavery, accused of attempted rape, thrown into prison, and forgotten for two more years after that. Yet God had not forgotten about him.

While you are reading this book right now, you may be experiencing a pit situation in your life, or some life circumstances may have left you feeling confined like a prison. Refuse to give up, God has a more excellent way for you, His plan is still in effect for you.

It was God's plan all along to take Joseph from the pit to the palace. Whatever your adversity, remember God is with you. He knows how to get you from your pit to your palace; and your dreams will become reality right on schedule just as He has planned it.

After interpreting Pharaoh's dreams, God blessed Joseph beyond his greatest expectations.

"Thou shalt be over my house, and according unto thy word shall all my people be ruled: only in the throne will I be greater than thou" Genesis 41:40 (KJV).

Probably, there were times with Joseph when it looked like his dreams would never be realized. The door seemed sealed shut, but God opened them.

As it was with Joseph, so it must be with us. His faith and his trust were completely in God who is in charge of closed doors.

Chapter 4

Have You Worn Your Genes Lately?
(The Genomics Revolution)

"In the beginning God created the heavens and the earth. And the earth was without form, and void: and darkness was upon the face of the deep. And the Spirit of God moved upon the face of the waters" *Genesis 1:1-2 (KJV)*. Genesis is the book of beginnings. It describes the beginning of all things pertaining to life here on earth; people, animals, plant life, and the heavenly bodies (the sky, solar system, and planets).

From the book of Genesis to the book of Revelation we read the story of mankind how he began in right standing with his creator and then committed high treason in the Garden of Eden. From there we can see man going through life as if on a roller coaster of highs, lows resulting from his actions back in the garden. Although there is much written in the first few chapters of the book about the activities of mankind and the creation of the universe, the main character of the book is not at all man, nor about the universe, but about God. *"In the beginning God..."* (Genesis 1:1). If God had not been there, nothing else could have come forth. He is the one who spoke all things into existence by the power of His word. God made man in His image and after His likeness. Mankind was given knowledge and the ability to create many things from material on earth provided by his creator; but only God can create something from nothing.

In Genesis chapter 1 and verse 1, the word "created" in Hebrew is *bara*, which means to dispatch. It conveys the thought of creating something out of nothing. While in *Genesis chapter 1 and verse 7*, the word *"made"* is Asa. The emphasis is on fashioning the thing that has been created. God has been fashioning the lives of mankind since He placed him here on the earth. One of the duties of man was to work, (or to tend the soil) keeping the garden.

"Then the Lord took the man and put him in the Garden of Eden to tend and keep it" (Genesis chapter 2 and verse 15). God's way for mankind and all of creation is to operate by the law of sowing and reaping, seedtime and harvest, giving and receiving. The seed sown will always produce a harvest because the law of God is that the seed sown will always multiply.

In Genesis chapter 1 and verse 1, God dispatched (sowed) the substance of His word. Verses 2 and 3 speak of God cultivating the word sown. Verses 4 through 10 are examples of multiplication, thus, making the atmosphere and the environment suitable for mankind. As you can see, God is not interested in subtraction but in multiplication. All that He says throughout the rest of chapter 1 deals with multiplication only.

Notice phrases like *"whose seed is in itself; or according to its kind"* (verses 11 and 12). Everything that God created and placed upon the earth has the seed of its kind within itself; a law that will never change. Throughout the ages, there have been people who have tried to change certain laws and standards that God has setup only to realize it was futile. To try and reverse what God has set in motion is like attempting to defy the law of gravity. If you jumped off of a seven-story building expecting to break the law of gravity, the only thing you would prove is that the law of gravity works. From the beginning God meant for His creation (mankind) to serve Him. Choosing not to live our lives according to His word only sets the stage for disaster. Disobedience to the laws of God and of Christ, as we have seen; can only lead to the fall of humanity, which leaves us as a prey to all kinds of deception both by the philosophy and worldly knowledge of mankind, as well as to devils and demonic forces, who bring false knowledge apart from the knowledge of God.

Increase of Knowledge

In the book of Daniel chapter 12 and verse 4 we read; *"But thou Daniel, shut up the words, and seal the book until the time of the end; many shall run to and fro, and knowledge shall increase."*

We are living in a time of increased knowledge. The depth of knowledge man has acquired has reached phenomenal proportions. It was by the Sovereignty of God's design from the beginning for man to increase in knowledge as well as in all areas of life. In our times this increase of knowledge that the Bible speaks of is so evident that sometimes it can be frightening.

"God is not a man, that He should lie, neither the son of man, that He should repent" Numbers Chapter 23 and verse 19. From the beginning God's expectation for this given knowledge was that men allow that knowledge to transfer over into trust. For men to trust that after God has made a promise to them, that He will always bring it to pass. Knowledge is a gift to us, and *"The gifts and callings of God are without repentance" according to Romans chapter 11 and verse 29.* This means that when He has given a gift, He never takes it back.

The "DEI Phenomenon"

Over the past few decades, we have witnessed a number of different phenomenon to arise.

DEI (Diversity, Equity and Inclusion) is one of many. This has arisen from different ethnic groups with the aim of changing society into something that God never meant. This group is made up of the so-called Transgender generation whose aim is to bring upon humanity a warped ideological lifestyle. On the surface it looks and sounds good, appearing to be something good thing to do, but the underlying effects would scar our children for many generations to come. It is one leg of a machine that leads a society into a socialistic lifestyle. Its origin is Satanic. It is a demonic ideology that is directly aimed at the destruction of a society, and to overthrow the lawful order of what God has established from the beginning. Such ideologies prevail in society when men refuse to live life by God's design. Only deception and ignorance are left.

I am convinced that many of them who are advocates of such lifestyles as DEI simply have not done their homework on the subject, while there are others who have yielded themselves freely over to the control of evil spirits.

There is no soft way to say it; all these things happen because of the sins of men. When people refuse to live according to the Bible; which is God's holy Word, they leave themselves open to the influence of evil spirits.

Thankfully God's Word provides the atonement for our sins. Jesus' blood that was shed on the cross at Calvary is that atonement. Whenever we have sinned in some way, thank God we can repent to the Lord, and He wipes the slate clean.

And we must be clear that to repent of something doesn't mean to feel and say I'm sorry only, but it means to change or to reverse one's actions; committing to going in the opposite direction.

The repentance spoken of (above) in the book of Romans shows us that once God has given us a gift, it's a one-way transaction; He never takes it back.

For mankind, knowledge can be acquired by natural and by spiritual means. Man is a spirit living in a physical body. We were designed to grow in knowledge. But we must be cautious that along with more knowledge comes the danger of becoming self-confident. One of the maladies of humanity is the temptation to feel self-sufficient. This was never meant to be. This kind of self-sufficiency leads into isolation from a healthy communication with our fellowman; but most importantly isolation from the Lord.

Often God has not answered our prayers because our self-sufficiency has weakened our relationship with Him. We missed the mark, and have begun putting our own brand of righteousness to work. It is so easy to come up with a self-interpretation of who we think God is; our own theology about the Bible, and how He works things in His universe. Indeed, God has given us the power to search out many mysteries to His creation, yet He is limitless, and His ways are past finding out. We know Him through the ways He has chosen to reveal Himself to us. Number one; being through His Word, the Holy Bible. In reality, the Bible is not just a book; it is the Spirit and the limitless mind of God, which is past finding out.

God created man on three planes of existence, in three dimensions, they are: spirit, soul, and body. This physical body is a house for the spirit and soul of man. God deals with man from the spiritual realm. It's only when God rules in our spirit can the soul and body be brought into subjection to the will of God. The soul and the body are nothing without the Spirit of God to take up residence within our spirit.

When Jesus came to earth, He made salvation available to all people. He saves all who will receive Him; and He keeps them by the power of the indwelling Holy Spirit.

"Therefore, if any man be in Christ, he is a new creature; old things have passed away; behold, all things have become new" (2 Corinthians chapter 5 and verse 17 KJV).

If a man or woman becomes new in Christ, then it is obvious that he or she was previously in a state that was unacceptable to God. He was in an unregenerate state (not yet redeemed). God calls it sin. Sin means missing the mark. Accepting Christ's sacrifice on the cross brings redemption. But as long as a man or woman has not repented of their sins and received Jesus as Lord, they appear naked before God and need to be clothed with His Spirit. In the eyes of God, apart from His Spirit, the flesh is dead. The human body, without the Spirit of God, can do about as much as a Boeing 747 on the ocean floor. It is absolutely useless.

Breaking the Genetic Code

We are living in the age of increased knowledge. You name it, man knows about it. It is the age the Bible calls "the last days." Yes, it is God's will that men should increase in knowledge, but He meant for the first degree of that knowledge to increase that men increase the knowledge of Jesus Christ; which is the beginning of wisdom. After all, all other knowledge is going to pass away according to *1 Corinthians 13:8c*. To know and to do what God's word says is the only thing that lasts forever.

In this age of increase in knowledge, it appears that scientists have now even learned how to break the genetic code of the human body. It is called Genomics. It is the study of the human genes, which, in part helps to determine a person's gender. With such knowledge many wonderful things could happen to the human race. Can you imagine the medical and scientific breakthroughs resulting from this kind of knowledge? Scientists may be able to find the cures for some of the worst diseases known to man. With advancements in scientific and medical circles, the world as we know it could change drastically, never to be the same again. Most of us are not scientists nor are we medical professionals. But as Christians, it is our responsibility to pray for those who have acquired such knowledge and who have such power in their hands. We need to lift our voices to God on their behalf, because *"The effectual fervent prayer of a righteous man avails much" James chapter 5 and verse 16 (KJV).*

There are at least two reasons why the body of Christ needs to pray for them. First of all, there are many people who have these gifts from God who recognize the great need to support global healing among men. Secondly, there are those who would only abuse the power that comes with such knowledge. These are usually those who are motivated by lust, greed, and many other forms of evil. Obviously, those who would abuse the power from such knowledge do not have man's best interest in mind. Can you imagine selling human genes for profit? Before you say; *"that is unthinkable"*, some people in the medical field are already inflicting a greater horror than this upon humanity by killing babies for money. It is called abortion. It is wrong, because a life is taken away every time a doctor performs an abortion.

Cloning

Some physicians and scientists have talked a lot about cloning over the past few years. To clone means to duplicate something. Some of them will be able to clone insects, animals, and who knows, maybe even human beings. But one thing is for certain; they will never be able to create and to breathe life into a human being. That is the one thing that makes each man and woman God's own unique property. Man can manipulate the physical body by playing with the human genes, but God alone is able to produce the spirit in a man.

Webster's dictionary definition for the word "gene" shows us that our genes are inherited from our parents. We are an extension of our parents. This means that we are made of the same stuff. Our genes carry what is called DNA. DNA is one of the nucleic acids that control the development of the body's cells; which is the basis of heredity in many organisms. Simply put, DNA is the fundamental building block of the human body. It determines who we are and where we came from.

Let's look at the word "heredity". It means transmitted from parent to offspring by birth. As it is in the natural, so it is when it comes to the spiritual. The life (spirit) within you and me came from God and God alone, which makes us His offspring. Humanity came forth from God. Even before creation itself He ordained which family each of us would be born into. It was all set before He formed Adam and Eve and placed them in the Garden of Eden. *"God sets the solitary in families" Psalm chapter 68 and verse 6 (KJV).* My point is this: that the spirit existed first, because *"God breathed into the nostrils of man, and man became a living soul" Genesis chapter 2 and verse 7 (KJV), only* then did the physical and natural part have life. There is an element of divine origin in each of us. God created the physical body and its many functions for his own purpose. Remember, I said earlier that the body is a house that the soul and spirit to dwell in. When Jesus comes into a person's life, He abides within their spirit. This being so, we should do in our bodies only what pleases God. Our bodies are the temple for His Holy Spirit to dwell in says *1 Corinthians chapter 3 and verse 13,* and its members (our body parts) belong to Jesus Christ *(1 Corinthians chapter 6 and verse 15 (KJV).* Enabled by the Holy Spirit, we are made acceptable for God's use alone. To assume authority over the body, with unbridled experiments, is the same as playing god.

We need to pray without ceasing for those who have acquired such knowledge concerning the human body. These scientists understand, at least to a degree, the mechanics of how the human body works. It would be so easy for those who are out for personal gain to begin to play god. Intellectual knowledge apart from the leading of the Holy Spirit is most dangerous. (You can read Proverbs chapter 30 on wisdom). Woe to those whose quest for power leads them to attempt to manipulate the plan of the living God. The quest for power without the wisdom of God only leads to deception, chaos, and destruction. God wants us to live in a loving and progressing fellowship with Him because He knows that flesh has no real life apart from His Holy Spirit.

John chapter 1 and verses 1-2 says; "In the beginning was the word, and the word was with God, and the word was God." He (Jesus) was in the beginning with God. Verse 4 says, *"In Him was life, and the life was the light of men."* When men walk with God long enough to develop a relationship with Him, they realize that He is the giver of life. But what most men fail to see is that God does not bring us into this world and then leave us to fend for ourselves. He is always present managing the lives of His people and the world He has created.

"And He is before all things, and in Him all things consist" (Colossians *chapter 1 and verse 17).*

In Greek, the word *consist* means joined to, committed to the care of. Jesus holds everything together, and is committed to maintaining the lives of men and women from conception until we return into His eternal presence. Your genes or your natural heredity declares who you are. From the beginning and by God's design, you and I have a determined end. We already have within us the ingredients (the DNA) that will bring us to what we shall be by the end of our lives. Included is what we are capable of accomplishing in our lifetime.

As it is in the natural, so it is in the spiritual. Godly men and women know that their future is not secured by their accomplishments, but by their obedience to the Lord Almighty who gives them the ability to accomplish what they do.

The physical body of man will never be complete without the Spirit of the living God. It's time for us to finally come to grips with what God has been saying to us all our lifetime. Without Him we can do nothing in this world. That is, nothing that will speak well for us in eternity. We were designed by God, and made in His image and likeness. Does that make us worth something? No, that makes us priceless. He is our life, and He has promised a hope and a bright future ahead of us, according to *Jeremiah chapter 29 and verse 11* (Read it).

As I previously mentioned, God created you and I as three-dimensional beings; which are spirit, soul and body. Each has its specific function given by God. Our spirit is where God meets us. His Spirit is where the life is, the quickening force that makes us alive. He is the enabler, and the power within us that makes the vehicle of our spirit, soul and body to function according to His perfect plan.

The soul being the seat of our intellect (i.e., our emotions and where decisions are made) is the connection point between our spirit and body. All of us have been guilty at some point of making a wrong choice or a bad decision that originated in our soul realm, only to suffer later for that decision.

When we learn to keep our guard up against emotional decisions, we will keep ourselves out of lots of trouble as we continue in obedience to God's Word. It does not mean that we won't make some mistakes, but He will enable us to exercise the discipline we need to avoid some pitfalls in life. Also, we receive wisdom to avoid giving soul solutions to problems that require answers from the Spirit of God. By yielding to the

Spirit of God, He gives us power in the soul to resist evil, thus robbing the body (the will of the flesh) of its power to control our lives. Life is not in the soul nor in the body but in the Spirit of God who quickens (makes alive) our spirit. Because of Jesus' sacrifice on the cross, we are made the righteousness of God according to *Romans chapter 4 and verse 6.*

God created us and He knows everything there is to know about His people. When all is said and done and men have exhausted their efforts of attempting to exploit God's creation, they will have to accept the undeniable truth that God is in control, He cannot be manipulated, and He will have the last word.

In John chapter 6 and verse 38, the scripture says: *"when Jesus came into the world He came to do the will of His father because He came from the father."*

As Christians, we are His children and we must do what pleases Him. We are part of His family because we have His spiritual genetics. Read Genesis chapter 2, and verse 7.

Learning to Walk with God

Now what about the life you've been living?

Think about the trail you have blazed over the past years. As you look back, are you proud of what you can see? Can you say *"I know it is well with me"* or do you have to admit it that you've been pretending and playing the game that so many play, which is apart from the reality of who you are. All who goes down that road only fool themselves.

Now, do you know the Lord as your personal Savior? Have you been observing others as they talk about Him, and you keep saying maybe I'll do it tomorrow? You may have said; that's not for me. Conversely, you may already be a Christian but you have not been living up to the commitment you once made to Jesus. Stop right here. Put everything else aside and take the next few moments and experience the joy of getting to know Christ, or getting to know Him all over again. Just simply say this prayer, "Lord I need you. I am lost without you, and I am helpless apart from you. Forgive me for my sins, and I receive you as my Savior and Lord in the name of Jesus, Amen."

I want to encourage you now to rise up and to put on your garment of righteousness.

Put it on, it is still in style. You cannot be righteous without the King of righteousness. Put on Christ, His genes fit you perfectly.

While men and women are running back and forth increasing in knowledge and being busy about things other than Christ, the stage is being set for our eternity. Don't waste any more time, it is too valuable to let it slip away. Natural genes identify us for where we've come from and to whom we belong. We must be properly dressed for the bridegroom and keeper of our souls to recognize our apparel when He returns. He will be expecting to receive back from us who are born again, that which He has put in our possession.

"And when the king came in to see the guests, he saw there a man which had not on a wedding garment: And he said unto him, friend, how did you came in hither not having a wedding garment? And he was speechless. Then said the king to the servants, bind him hand and foot, and take him away, and cast him into outer darkness; There shall be weeping and gnashing of teeth. For many are called, but few are chosen" Matthew chapter 22 and verses 11-14 (KJV).

As faith without works is dead; so is the body without the Spirit is dead according to James chapter 2 and verse 17 (KJV).

If we are living by the natural principles of life only, we are not really living. Living by God's word is how we get fully dressed and where life is made complete. It is about time we took a closer look into the instruction manual of life (the Bible) to find out if we are properly dressed for the coming divinely orchestrated occasion. Real life is not found in acquiring enough knowledge by probing into the unknown mysteries of our world, nor trying to satisfy the senses through the explorations of curiosity. But it is found in coming to know that God is our source. Putting on His righteousness and obeying only His commands is where we can find and live the abundant life that He promises. Once we are willing and obedient in doing His will, we have put on the right attire, and now we are really dressed for eternity. Therefore, I conclude by respectfully asking you; *"Have you worn your genes lately?"*

Chapter 5

Anointed With No Money

Earlier in chapter four, we saw that God gave man an occupation to work and to keep the Garden of Eden. Nowadays, when we mention work, some people do not want to hear about it. They feel that after forty hours on the job they want to keep their minds clear of that word. Perhaps most of us, at least to some degree, feel the same way. However, to be able to work is actually a blessing that God incorporated as a part of man's existence. When we work, we earn money to provide for our families and to fund the spreading of the gospel.

Strangely enough, God relates our money with our life. As we exert our energy, time and sweat each week on our job, we are not only giving our employer and that company our time but also a part of ourselves. We may not care much for the job we have, and perhaps we have a good reason for that. Maybe the boss acts like a snob or a co-worker doesn't like us. Whatever the situation, we must see beyond the distractions and see our job as help made available by God. It is a resource to support us so that we can be a blessing in the work of allowing God's Kingdom to come on earth as it is in Heaven. The job is not our source, but a resource. God is our source.

"But thou shall remember the Lord thy God: For it is He that gives thee power to get wealth, that He may establish His covenant which He swear unto thy fathers, as it is this day" Deuteronomy chapter 8 and verse 18 (NKJV). We must realize that God has provided all that we have. He has made us stewards (one who manages another's concerns or affairs)

over what we possess, everything that is a part of our life; including our finances. A steward is also expected to be faithful.

"Bring ye all the tithes into the storehouse, that there may be meat in my house, and prove me now herewith, says the Lord of hosts, if I will not open you the windows of heaven, and pour you out a blessing, that there shall not be room enough to receive it" Malachi chapter 3 and verse10 (KJV).

The tithe belongs to God. Give to God first of all what belongs to Him. Then the stage is set for success. God trusts us enough to put finances in our hands and lets us make the decision to honor Him in how we handle them.

It's a sad thing to know that some people expect to prosper with God's blessings, but they don't want to do it God's way. They have a plan of their own. And when it comes to finances, I'm surprised at their ideas on how to manage them. There was a time in my life when I was trying to straighten out my financial situation. A friend of mine advised that I visit an acquaintance of his who was as he said; a financial consultant. The consultant claimed to be a Christian. As I sat talking with him I was seeking the best strategy to get me back on course, when he made this statement: *"Mr. Johnson, why don't you eliminate the tithe?"* Well, needless to say, at that moment I knew what my next move would be. I got out of there as quickly as I could.

Now I could have agreed with him and figured out other ways to straighten out my finances, and begin to prosper and accumulate lots of things without giving a tithe. However, I realized that I would not experience real happiness with what I would acquire, plus, I would not be able to hold on to it. I would have worked hard to get lots of things but I would not be satisfied with them because my priorities were not in line with God's word. Prosperity gotten apart from God's way brings temporary results.

Proverbs chapter 3 and verses 9-10 tells us to *"honor the Lord with your substance, and with the first fruits of all your increase: so shall your barns be filled with plenty, and your presses shall burst out with new wine."*

This way of prosperity comes because of obedience to God, who promises to reward us in this life, but also to yield eternal dividends. God's way is the right way. To be able to prosper is a gift from God. When we depend on Him, He enables us to prosper; resulting in blessings enough to bless others. Ecclesiastes chapter 10 and verse 19 says, *"...but money answers all things."* The New King James Key Word Study Bible side note says; it "makes glad the life." God has made the money system as a resource not only to provide for our families, but also to fund the spreading of the gospel.

In this age of modern technology, there are get-rich-quick schemes and other ways to get us to spend our money. The way the world system works is, if we have money, we have power. While we know that taking care of our families is one of the most important reasons God gave us money, we are also held responsible to use our finances to support the work of the Church as He continues to build His kingdom on earth.

This is why it is so important for us as the body of Christ to come out of debt and stay out.

I realize that we are all indebted to someone. Each month some of us are indebted to paying the bank that holds our mortgage, while others are committed to paying our car note. These are debts normal to life in most countries. However, what I'm talking about is that outstanding credit card debt from frivolous spending that's been there so long, you think that it's a pet. There are also those financial debts you owe people that are not recorded on public records. Are you concerned about them? I don't say this to condemn anyone, but simply to say; remaining in outstanding debt can hinder us from living a prosperous life. It will stifle our ability to shoulder the responsibilities we are to provide for our families. And, remaining outstanding debt can also snuff out our efforts to successfully finance the spreading of the gospel.

In this age of accelerated knowledge and the mega church, it is easy to find prosperity preachers all around. However, to preach prosperity and to be prosperous are entirely two different things.

"Beloved, I wish above all things that you may prosper and be in health, even as thy soul prospers - 3 John chapter 1 and verse 2 (KJV).

God wants us to preach the gospel. Prosperity is included in the preaching of the gospel as we sow and reap and give tithes. To be effective in this area, we must live it as well as preach it. We are expected to prosper in this area our finances.

Let me ask you, *"Where is your money?"* God relates your money to your life, and He must have a good reason to do so. Yes, money is a resource instituted by God as part of His blessing plan for us that we may be a blessing in this physical world. However, did you know that money (a natural substance) is compared in ways to the spiritual realm? For instance, when you purchase an item at your local department store and do not take it home with you on the first visit, you normally lay it away by leaving a down payment and leaving it at the store. It is a guarantee that tells the proprietor that you will return with the remaining balance to complete the purchase at a later date.

II Corinthians chapter 5 and verse 5 tell us; *"Now he that hath wrought us for the self same thing is God, who also hath given unto us the earnest of the Spirit."*

The words "God has wrought" in Greek mean: bought or purchased us for immortality. The word earnest in the lexical aids of the New Testament is arrabon; which means earnest money, a pledge, a down payment. It stands for part of the price and is paid beforehand to confirm the bargain. Spiritually, speaking; the Holy Spirit is the down payment on the full purchase or reward that awaits us in God's presence when this life is over.

The pivotal point in the area of finances in my life was after I got married. I had financial struggles in my life that I couldn't seem to overcome until God used my wife to get in my face so to speak. She told me things that deep down I already knew, but I just needed the right person to say it to me. She said: You will either sink or swim, it is your choice. I knew it was time to change that.

After that I learned that when God is about to bring about change in your life some of the weirdest things can begin to happen. He creates opportunities for our faith to grow.

Now I had a greater determination to take the bull by the horns. I wanted to be out of debt, and I wanted it yesterday! Then the most heart breaking and disappointing thing happened. I lost my job. The same woman who had encouraged me to come out of debt was not working at the time, and there was no income in sight. Talk about being in a place where I needed to learn to trust God!

I learned more valuable lessons about money and trust in God's faithfulness during those times than I had learned probably in all the other years of my life. I was faced with the choice of either to die of worry, or learn to trust God. We were blessed by the Lord, and most of the time our needs were being met, but I had no money, I was broke. Much of this was due to a combination of things, besides frivolous spending, and not handling my money wisely. As I ministered to others, I saw God do miraculous things in their lives. I prayed for them and they were healed, their lives were changed, and they were set free. I was anointed for spiritual things while in the area of finances I had big problems. I was blessing others, but I was broke; that was not God's best for me. I had a lesson to learn about properly handling my finances. So I started sowing my financial seed according to what the Bible says about it.

A seed can be compared to a down payment on a harvest. The burial and resurrection of Jesus' body can be compared to a down payment on many souls that will be resurrected.

"But as it is written, eye hath not seen, nor ear heard, neither have entered into the heart of man the things which God hath prepared for them that love Him" 1 Corinthians chapter 2 and verse 9 (KJV).

God has prepared so much for us to enjoy after this life is over, but He also expects us to enjoy life here on earth using every resource He has made available to us, and that includes our money as well. Yes, you heard me right, even properly handling our finances is a way we honor The Lord.

"The secret things belong to the Lord our God: But the things which are revealed belong unto us, and our children forever, that we may do all the words of this law" Deuteronomy chapter 29 and verse 29 (KJV).

Finances are of necessity to the Lord's work. He uses it as He ushers in His Kingdom here on earth. He expects us to work for it, but he also expects us to learn to make it work for us. I remember spending years of my life in ministry as a pastor and not having sufficient finances at times. My wife and I struggled for a while before we became successful in ministry. Some of our difficulties were the result of not properly handling our finances. In order to successfully manage what belonged to God, we needed to have our finances in order. We should give the tithe first, because it belongs to God. During those days we learned to seek God's face in prayer for guidance for our home, and to properly handle our finances first for our household. As we did, God gave us wisdom, and by his power He helped us to turn everything around, and we prospered in everything we did for Him.

During my early years of ministry, I learned that I could be greatly anointed and broke at the same time. That is not what God wants for us, He wants us to have both; anointed and to be prosperous. The anointing makes things happen for us in the Spirit. But money can make things happen for us in the natural. God wants us to have both. God calls out men and women and puts His anointing upon their lives to minister His word, to pray for the sick, and to do many other great things for Him. However, you can be an anointed spiritual giant whose wallet belongs to a dwarf if you don't have control of your finances. One of the worst tragedies in an individual's life or an organization, especially in the church, is never gaining control of one's finances. It takes finances to fund the Gospel. But we cannot properly manage the ministry's finances until we have successfully learned how to manage our own finances. If we want to have godly success, we must make sure our own finances are in order before attempting to manage the church's finances.

Debt puts us into bondage. But when our finances are in order, we have freedom; freedom that gives us a voice in society with connections literally to the world; and beyond this simple truth we have peace of mind. Also, we will have the two-fold blessing of being in a position to help others who may have one kind of need or another. People tend to have the utmost respect for us when we exercise wisdom in handling our finances.

This puts us in control when it comes to selling and purchasing. It also puts us in a position where we can give sound financial advice to those who may need it, plus others will be more inclined to listen to what we have to say.

God expects His children to be wise in managing their finances. Our finances belong to Him, and He will hold us accountable for how we have used them.

"And it came to pass, that when He was returned, having received the kingdom, then He commanded these servants to be called unto him, to whom he had given the money" Luke chapter 19 and verse 15. "And he said unto him, out of your own mouth will I judge thee, thou wicked servant. You knew that I was an austere man, taking up that I laid not down, and reaping that I did not sow" Luke chapter 19 and verse 22.

As godly men and women, we are called to a life of integrity. We must always be aware of the on-looking world that is watching to see a true representation of Christ in our stewardship. As Christians we can sometimes focus more on the spiritual side of things, and neglect with little emphasis on the natural side. Now granted, we are spiritual and we should be spiritually minded. But when we fail to properly manage our finances we won't be going very far in life. Jesus must be Lord over the physical as well as the spiritual part of man. He expects you and I to exercise integrity by applying the godly principles found in His word.

Chapter 6

Ordinary Champions

By God's design, life is to be lived in such a way that one Generation passes on the right values that will sustain the next. He does this in part through the preaching of the Gospel, the good news of Jesus.

But a generation is not changed simply because a minister decides to give a message that fits in with the times. It is God's message that affects change in each generation. His plan exceeds the plans of men. He accomplishes it though methods we probably would not think of using, yet He uses people to accomplish it.

Have you ever wondered why God uses some people who seem the most unlikely to succeed in carrying out His mission? He is the source of life, and He has resources that you and I have no knowledge of. We can read in the Bible about great victories won against overwhelming odds through seemingly insignificant people in unconventional ways. For instance: What about a group of priests and soldiers marching around the wall of Jericho? They were commanded to circle the city once a day for six days. Then, on the seventh day to march seven times, after which they were to shout. The walls fell down flat! Read the book of Joshua chapter 6 and verses 12-21 (KJV). They were men, but they were God's army, God's champions. They were chosen to do what seemed in the eyes of men to be impossible. God is still raising champions today. By the power of God, men rise to the task and become achievers and heroes. In a word, Champions.

In today's world, Hollywood keeps turning out the world's brand of them. A champion is a person of great accomplishment; one who has done some notable tasks in accomplishing something that society classifies as extra ordinary. Champions can influence and even motivate others beyond their perceived abilities, igniting responses that cause change even in the lives of them who seem the most unlikely.

God makes champions. But the way He does it is by far different from our way of thinking. On the natural side, men become champions for the thrill of the goal and for the admiration of other men. But God raises men and women and makes them champions to affect change in generations. He raises men and women of integrity who will lead others to put their trust in Jesus the Savior.

To Rescue a Generation

"The earth is the Lord's and the fullness thereof; the world and they that dwell in it."

"This is the generation of them that seek Him, that seek thy face O Jacob" Psalm chapter 24 and verses 1 and 6 (KJV).

God is interested in Generations. He is concerned about your Generation. He oversees the affairs of mankind as He looks for those who will listen to His voice. Just as He watched over and sustained past civilizations, He is touching the present Generations. He will sustain them because of His great love for them. And because He is the author and creator of them, He comes to visit you in your times. From Baby Boomers, to Gen X, to millennials, to Generations Y and Z, and on to Generation Alpha; God has been active behind the scenes working for the good of them who love Him.

God has looked upon these in search of them who have a servant's heart. They may not realize it, but God is watching them because He has a remnant among them with great potential to do exploits in His hand. Exploits I say; in His hand, because He has the power to change their lives from chaos to calm, from confusion to peace, and from having no direction to having their steps ordered by the Lord. Apart from their challenges to figure out how they fit into society; God has given them the power to excel in the world, and to become a greater generation of champions than the previous one. Each Generation is born with potential that is more than adequate for the times they are in.

For the good of them, God will create a platform for them to stand upon in life because He is in the business of making champions.

A generation of people are changed by the word of God. It is a word that fits into every season of life. God gives the message that will change each generation according to His own plans. He does it in ways we likely would never expect. He doesn't scout the earth looking for the great and powerful or the excellent and the wonderful, although He could if it pleased Him.

But throughout the history of Biblical events, we can see that often God used ordinary people like you and me to accomplish great things for Him.

"Because the foolishness of God is wiser than the wisdom of men; and the weakness of God is stronger than the strongest among men" according to 1 Corinthians chapter 1 and verse 25 (NKJV).

God raises up kingdoms and He brings them down, so He is well able to make men and women into whom He wants them to be. He calls a sinner out of the world, transforms the life, and calls him/her the righteousness of God; while man making his very best effort could never earn the right to be called righteous before God. We were sinners at birth because of our first parents Adam and Eve who sinned in the Garden of Eden. Jesus alone was the sufficient sacrifice to save a world of sinners. And why? It is because of a Love that goes beyond all human understanding. And a love that reaches so deep that it defies all the trophies of man's knowledge. The love of Jesus lifts the downtrodden up to a place of honor; and He restores whatever thieves have taken away.

A champion raised by God is one who is obedient, one who has made the Lord his God. This is a real champion. We can see many examples throughout the Bible how the Lord worked righteousness and subdued kingdoms using ordinary people from different backgrounds and different ethnic groups. The power of God is able to melt the stoniest heart and to bring men and women into fellowship with Him.

Raising Champions

"And Saul, yet breathing out threatening and slaughter against the disciples of the Lord, went to the high priest, and desired of him letters... that he might bring them bound unto Jerusalem" Acts chapter 9 and verses 1-2 (KJV).

"...and putting his hands on him said, brother Saul, the Lord, even Jesus, that appeared unto you in the way as thou came, hath sent me, that thou might receive thy sight, and be filled with the Holy Ghost" Acts 9 and verse 17 (KJV).

Saul was a notorious and an injurious person. He persecuted the Christians of the early church. However, he was not beyond the reach of the Master's hand.

No matter where we are in life, God is able to bring us out of the worst of situations into right standing and a relationship with Him.

What a champion God made out of the man Saul. After Saul's conversion, his name was changed to Paul. The name Paul means "small, or humble", which speaks in volume to his transformation. Under the inspiration of the Holy Spirit, he became the writer of most of the New Testament books of the Holy Bible.

God is still making champions from ordinary people today who will worship Him and heed His call. He seeks for those who will worship Him in spirit and in truth according to John chapter 4 and verse 23 (KJV). God empowers men and women whom He can use to be Instrumental in shaping the lives of others for eternity. Although He knows our flaws and failures, He chooses to use imperfect people through whom He can work His will and bring glory to His name. We need only to give our lives to the Master and to make ourselves available for His use. There is a champion in you. But the question is: Are you making yourself available, or are you trying to run away from the one who is in the process of making champions for eternity? Although God does this through unconventional ways, He has been doing this since the beginning of time. We dare not take lightly God's method of fashioning future champions.

And there is a price to pay in becoming the kind of champion God raises. Those who would become champions by the hand of God are the ones who are willing to be molded, prodded, and shaped by His hand. At times, that may call for putting up with some things we may not like. That could mean anything from suffering some hardship, to simply being accountable to others. Suffering is a part of our heritage as children of God. You say, *Say what?* That's right. Suffering is a part of our heritage as children of God.

"And if children, then heirs; heirs of God, and joint heirs with Christ; if so be that we suffer with him, that we may be also glorified together" Romans Chapter 8 and verse 17 (KJV).

Suffering teaches us patience and when we patiently wait for the Lord, His knowledge opens our eyes to how this life is designed for us to live. It teaches us not to live just for and to ourselves, but to serve others, and to be accountable to others. Whether that's being accountable to those in leadership over us, or simply out of respect to some family member, we must be held accountable for our words and actions. Lives lived unaccountable to anyone leads to uncontrollable sin. By design we were created to worship our creator. Our hearts must be right before the Lord, especially as we bring our petitions to Him. We cannot presumptuously come before His presence with the wrong attitudes or motives because in such a mindset we are unprepared.

Now I know that people become offended when we talk like that, but God sees us through eyes of holiness and He cannot tolerate sin or a sinful attitude as we approach Him. Many times, the wrong attitude can be the result of some hardship the individual may be facing at the time. However, we must remember that hardships and blessings go hand-in-hand as we live the Christian life. The sooner we come to grips with this great truth, the happier and the more victorious we will be as we live for the Lord.

Just as leaders are made and not born, so are Champions. Champions are shaped in the crucible of afflictions, and the furnace of testing on the battlefield that challenges their faith. I said in an earlier chapter that it is not faith if it has not been tested by the fiery trial. But don't become discouraged when I speak of the trial of your faith. Trials have always been the tools God uses in the making of champions.

When God Goes On Vacation

"Beloved, think it not strange concerning the fiery trial which is to try you, as though some strange thing happened to you. But rejoice, in as much as ye are partakers of Christ's sufferings: that when his glory shall be revealed, you may be glad also with exceeding joy" (1 Peter chapter 4 and verse 12-13 (KJV).

Anyone whom God is training in the school of Champions has to pass through what I call God's vacation period. This is a time on your Christian walk when it seems that you are walking alone, and God has taken a vacation leaving you in charge.

I mean those times when you pray and God doesn't respond. You can understand it when He holds off from answering you for a few days or weeks, but now it has turned into months and even years. Now that mountain-moving sermon that you've been preaching to others seems to be insufficient before the mountain that's standing in your path. You speak to it, but there is no apparent response. Well, take courage my friend; God is up to something! The rewards of having faith in God to accomplish what is needed reach far beyond our comprehension.

"And Jesus said unto them, because of your unbelief: for verily I say unto you, if you have faith as a grain of mustard seed, ye shall say unto this

mountain, remove hence to yonder place; and it shall remove; and nothing shall be impossible unto you" Matthew chapter 19 and verse 26 (KJV).

My next statement may sound contradictory to most people's understanding of how faith works.

What if every time you or I speak to a situation or problem (our mountain), without any challenge, it is instantly solved, or the mountain suddenly disappears and it gives us no resistance to fight, it just easily melts or slides out of our way? Where is the faith in that? That is not faith at all.

God knows that we cannot experience victory over a mountain that has never refused to move. God builds up our faith in Him as He makes champions out of us. What I mean is that often our idea of faith building is wrong. My faith is made stronger only when it is challenged by my mountain's "no" answer. But my persistent declaration of "yes in the name of Jesus" is what renders the "no" answer powerless. Faith that has never been challenged is not really faith at all, and God requires our response of faith in His process of creating Champions. So take courage my brothers and sisters! God is up to something wonderful!

Admit it, Just Say You Blew it!

There have been times in my life when God gave me assignments to carry out. Although I was honored to think that He would love me enough to choose me for the task, I must admit that many times I failed before I completed it. Thankfully God gives grace during those times. He allows us to come to the reality of our helplessness apart from putting complete trust in Him. There was a time in my ministry that I felt like I was standing still; it seemed like I wasn't making any progress. So I did a self- examination. I like to call it a spiritual checkup. After praying about it, God made me aware of the problem.

Whenever He had spoken anything to my heart, Satan would come afterward to discourage me. Instead of declaring the word of God over my situation, each time I would let those feelings of discouragement overwhelm me, it was a big mistake, thus, I was left with a sad heart. This caused many setbacks in my life. I was focusing more on the flesh and how bad things looked rather than trusting God and declaring His word.

Many people in the body of Christ today have come to a halt in their walk with God because of some mistake, a bad decision, or some other kind of setback. They blew it along the way and felt like it was over. But I have found that the quickest way to recovery is to admit to God that you blew it. Confess that you did not do it right and that you need His help. God is waiting for you to simply pray that prayer, so He can get you back on course, and continue your journey.

It is Satan's job to get you and me to feel like we do not measure up, or that we are now out of God's graces. But Satan is a liar and the accuser of the brethren. God is not angry with you. He has said that He will never leave you nor forsake you.

Let's take a look at the life of the Apostle Peter. He was just an ordinary citizen like you and me. Not one who had a house full of trophies. He was simply a fisherman by trade (Matthew chapter 4 and verse 18). Jesus called Peter into ministry and told him that he would now fish for men. However, after his meeting with Jesus, Peter did not immediately follow Him. Peter went back to Capernaum and continued his vocation as usual. He was waiting for further instruction. Jesus called him, knowing the total man. Jesus could see the man inside and out. He knew Peter's thoughts and his ways. Jesus was aware of Peter's attitude and his temper, but He called him anyway, and the reason is that Jesus knew the man's heart. We can rest assured that God never looks for perfect people to accomplish His purposes. But whomever He calls, He does set the standard by which they are to live. He is in the business of perfecting (making holy) the ones He has called. Jesus would certainly accomplish what He had purposed to do in Peter's life, but not without some challenges to Peter. Challenges that would lead to the changes needed to accomplish God's will for his life. The call was now on Peter's life, but the transformation had not yet taken place. God raises godly men and women in the midst of adversities. Peter would learn this truth through Jesus Christ who is the enabler.

By the end of Peter's life, he had become nothing short of the Champion God had determined for him to be. In Matthew chapter 26 and verse 33, Peter declared that he would never be offended because of Jesus. However, in verses 69-74 of the same chapter, we see him denying Jesus three times. It is easy to say to the Lord that we will be faithful to Him no matter what. But faithfulness can be realized only in adversity and under pressure; which demands a decision on our part. Peter had now spoken unwisely, and later went back on his word.

When it comes to trials, I have learned this one thing; that what convinces other people that we are genuine followers of Christ is how we respond in the heat of trial.

Faith is one directional. In order to know how strong it is, it must be tested. Our response to it will either move us forward, or we will suffer a setback.

The trial of our faith gives us sure footing and stability in whatever life may bring.

If you can believe it, such a precious moments as the trial of our faith is what God waits for from His children. What He wants to be able to say about you and me is: *That's my child, and I know he* (or she) *loves me; they trust me regardless.*

Perhaps, like Peter, you have made some wrong choices or bad decisions because of the pressures of life, and like Peter, you feel like you have already failed before you could get started. Maybe you feel like you have not reached your goals in life as you thought you would, and you feel discouraged about continuing on. Well, whatever your situation, I want to encourage you to stop and think. It is always too soon to quit. You must open your ears, pray and listen for the voice of God. As bad as things may seem, if you love the Lord, conditions are right for great miracles to happen. This could be just the right moment for major breakthroughs in your life. God uses these trials to mold champions. It is not pleasant while we are going through, but we must learn to allow God the time to strip away all the crud and everything that will be of no use to Him. Only then are we equipped for new levels of service for Him. Our victories are won, not in the absence of trouble, but in the presence of power. Don't waste your afflictions. Let each of them be stepping-stones to your next level of grace in Christ. Instead of allowing past events to dictate to you what the outcome of your life will be, learn to live your life with your sights set on Jesus who gave us our greatest example of overcoming; He is the author and finisher of your faith. God has already secured our future according to Jeremiah Chapter 29, verse 11 (KJV).

Peter had blown it, but Jesus' plan for him would not be altered. Peter's mistakes wouldn't change a thing. The world would still see The Lord do what only He does best. That is, to take the ordinary and create a champion.

For me, one of the most encouraging verses in the Bible is found in St. Mark chapter 16 and verse 7. Here the angel of the Lord said to the women who came to the tomb where Jesus had been laid. It says: "But go your way, tell his disciples and Peter that he goes before you into Galilee: there shall you see him, as he said unto you."

Notice the statement: "…tell his disciples *and Peter*". Although the angel of the Lord makes this announcement, we know without a doubt it is really Jesus who is saying, tell Peter you are still mine, I have great plans for you, and I will meet you later to complete what I have started in you.

Maybe you have blown it by making a wrong decision that has left you feeling like God has changed His mind, and forgotten about you. Well, God is not through with you yet. Delayed does not mean denied. Sometimes God puts us on the shelf and waits for His perfect timetable to roll our season into view. He will fulfill what He has promised. So be diligent and continue to live faithfully for His cause. There is a place He is aiming to bring you to and, as He promised Peter, He has promised you and I; He will meet us there.

Peter had denied his Lord three times earlier. However, in St. John chapter 21 and verses 15-19, Jesus asked Peter three times if he loved Him. Now Peter had a second opportunity to examine his own heart before answering. Jesus revealed to Peter His own death and how He would glorify God. Then Jesus concluded, "Follow me".

Peter turned out to be one of the New Testament's greatest leaders of the church, read Acts chapters 1-12. They include the New Testament books that bear his name, first and second Peter. His life is an example of how God raises ordinary champions. God is faithful, and He will always accomplish His purpose in our lives.

Moses is another man whom God raised up and made a champion. Remember how Moses made excuses when God commanded him to go to Egypt and tell Pharaoh to let the children of Israel go? In the book of Exodus Chapter 3, verse 11, Moses said to God, "…But who am I to go to Pharaoh?" In chapter 4 and verse 1, he was still reluctant to obey God's call to go to Egypt. Moses did not think that he was the right person for the task. But for fear of Jehovah, he finally obeyed. Gathering his family and belongings, he began his journey to Egypt.

God is completely acquainted with every man; He knows our capabilities because He created us. Moses didn't think he could lead Israel out of Egypt, and he was right. But he would do it through the power of God. Moses was only looking at what he thought he could not do, but God knew what He Himself could do through Moses. Moses could only see through eyes of flesh. He only saw a weak man with a speech impediment. But God was looking at a champion who, by the power of His hand, would resound into history past and reverberate into future generations; and give a whole new meaning to the words, "Have faith in God." God accomplished His purpose with Moses.

How many times have you and I let circumstances convince us that Jesus has changed His mind about us? Have you decided that He is no longer interested in using you because things didn't happen at the time you thought they would? Jesus never forgets the promises He has made to them whom He has called. With the Word of God, godly men gird themselves with the strength that God has made available for the task. Although you may be an ordinary person in ordinary or even extraordinary circumstances, you must be aware of this great truth; that God has something greater in mind for you. You are a champion in the making. Did you know that the champions of faith that God is bringing forth in the earth in these days have come through the fires of adversity? God himself takes them through trials producing patience and strength; preparing them for what He is about to do in these closing hours of grace?

When significant breakthrough and a notable work of God is near to be revealed, He causes a stirring in the spirit of men, because His blessings are on the way. At such times, the promises He has made may seem like they have taken a turn and headed in the opposite direction, and you're left feeling like God has forsaken you. During these times, we experience what I call the desert place of our walk with Jesus Christ. These are the times when some things that once seemed perfectly normal and in line with God's plan for our life, suddenly seem to make no sense. This is when we must learn to take courage, my friend, because we are experiencing Gethsemane (the place of agony). This is the place where Jesus often resorted to pray, (read Luke chapter 22 and verses 39-42) and found comfort. Gethsemane also became the place where He agonized just before going to the cross. This says to us that we will not only enjoy the good times and blessings of Christ in our lives, but there will be times of suffering also. II Timothy chapter 2 and verse 12 reminds us: *"If we suffer, we shall also reign with him"*. We need only to learn to view our suffering as an avenue to the next level of blessing and closeness to the Savior. God will never come short of performing the promises He has made to His people. He has declared that what He has spoken must shortly come to pass because the time is at hand.

God is working on no small thing concerning you. He has big plans for your life that shall soon be revealed in His timing. Hold tight, gird up your loins, we're in this for the long haul, so stand firm! It takes time for the Master craftsman to develop His masterpiece. But when He is finished, there shall stand nothing short of a Champion. The purpose for these moments of preparation is to bring forth disciples for Jesus in order to affect change for good in generations to come. So be patient. God is busy within you. He is at work raising a champion. The essence of a champion is priceless, but there is a price to pay for championship. Sometimes that means suffering. Godly men are champions and they know that they cannot influence others for good apart from spending time with God. So arise to the task, and give yourself to the trainer. I guarantee, in so doing, you too will become a champion for the Lord.

The Three Dreams

Dream One

During my years in Ministry, I have been honored to serve as Pastor of three Churches. There was a time as Pastor of the second church, I had a series of three dreams that frightened me and troubled me greatly. In the first dream, I saw the church as children playing in a wide opened field. As they played, they did as most children do, they were pretending to be characters other than themselves. As they played, without realizing it, they wandered off into the forest. While having fun, suddenly there was a loud crashing sound near by which caused every child great alarm. As they turned to see the most frightening sight they had ever seen. They beheld five giant creatures larger than life. The children stood almost paralyzed with fear. It started when they saw a giant creature (purple in color) racing across the forest leveling the trees as it went. As they beheld, there appeared a second giant creature (greenish-grey in color) resembling a tyrannosaurus; in pursuit of the first creature with its jaw teeth showing as if to devour or destroy it.

I understand later that the purple-colored creature represented the great harlot in the earth, and the greenish grey-colored creature represented The Judgment of God.

If that was not overwhelming enough, the children turned around and saw a giant grey-colored locust headed in their direction. It went between two of the children as they hid behind two trees. One child, while peeking from behind the tree, saw a giant black widow spider positioned in their direction but only watching them. As they watched, they saw a second black widow spider as it lifted its leg to come forward.

The Locust represented pestilence, the first black widow spider represented warning, while the second spider represented death.

At this point when the second black widow lifted its leg to come forward, all the children ran with every ounce of strength they could muster. The first dream ended.

Dream Two

The following night, the second dream was a continuation of the first. One child, while at home with his parents, asked them "Did the children tell you what things we saw in the forest today?" His mother said "No, what things?" His father said; "I don't want to hear anything evil." The child proceeded to tell them what happened. The parents did not feel good at all about what they heard and became very restless. The dream ended.

Dream Three

The third night, the dream continued. I saw a man who opened his eyes to find himself standing in a harlot's house. God began to cause him to pass from room to room; allowing him to observe all the vile, and degrading things done in the harlot's chambers. He was devastated at the sight of it all. When he realized it, he began to say, "What is this? This is not where I live!"

Then suddenly a storm came up, and what a storm it was. It was like no storm I had ever seen before. The clouds in the heavens were black with a darkness I cannot put into words, and there was a form of lightning I had never seen before. The force of the wind showed God's power unleashed as I stood in awe and utter amazement to see the wind blow so strong that it took the flesh off of men's bones. Yet right in the midst of the storm, I looked down to the ground to see what seemed to be the most contradictory of all scenarios. I saw a man on his hands and knees crawling out of such vehement wind and storm, crawling with seemingly relentless determination to get free. The sensation I got in the dream was that God was giving him strength to do it. He crawled it seemed for miles until he crawled up the steps of a church; up the aisle and right up to the altar. He raised himself to the kneeling position on his knees, and with his hands lifted toward heaven he said "Lord I repent." Suddenly, with a loving fatherly yet stern tone of voice, I heard the Spirit of the Lord say, "This is what it will take, and I will receive nothing less!"

The three dreams spoke of the condition of the lives of many people in God's church.

Repentance has not gone out of style. God still requires men to acknowledge their transgressions and to confess their sins.

"If my people which are called by my name, shall humble themselves and pray, and seek my face, and turn from their wicked ways; then will I hear from heaven, and will forgive their sin, and will heal their land" II Chronicles chapter 7 and verse 14 (NKJV).

Throughout the history of the Bible, before God brought change among His people, He always called men to repentance. Even today, He is calling men to repent through prayer and seeking His face. For this end-time harvest to be reaped in the earth, God will send forth men and women with the fire of His Spirit who will carry His Word to the ends of the earth.

A Prophecy

This Millennium will bring great changes to the body of Christ. The stage is set for global changes. There is a shifting in the spiritual realm. A time of catastrophic movement orchestrated from the heavens because the time is at hand. God's timetable has rolled around to its designated point for certain things purposed by God to happen regarding His church. Hear what the Spirit says to the church: *"For a long time I have held my peace while the enemy played with the minds of my holy ones. But now will I arise to defend my bride, my chosen, my called out ones. The afflictions of my people shall not be wasted. For my ears are open to their cry. And when they call unto me, I will come near unto them and will not hesitate as in former days. But beware, I will come with holiness, so gird up your selves with strength, and clothe yourselves with righteousness. You who have been termed forsaken will I gather under my wings for my own and no one shall make you afraid. I will deal with pastors and many in leadership who have caused many to stumble and become discouraged.*

I hate robbery and offense. I will bring down the one who is lifted high in his pride, and I will exalt the humble man to a place of honor. This generation has been to me as those in the day of trouble when the children came to the birth, but there was no strength to bring forth II Kings 19:3 (KJV). But I will be your mid-wife. I will deliver you. Bring forth! Bring forth! The Lord will crush Satan under your feet. My whirlwind has gone out into the heavens, and my battle bow will affect changes in the earth. The transfer is taking place on behalf of my anointed. And you will walk in the realm of the Spirit that I have called you into," says the Lord.

Chapter 7

God's Prize Possession

The Family

The family is the foundation upon which all of human society rests. Who could ever give it the clearest instruction and the best advice but God alone? Its foundation was established on love, the love of God. God's love is described as "Ahaba" (Hebrew) and Agape (Greek), and it is the highest characteristic of God. The establishment of the family was meant to be an expression of the heart of God for His people. Generally, the world has come up with some ideas of what they think it is, and called it love. The God kind of love cannot be realized or even defined in a person's life apart from Him. The love of God is more than kindness or benevolence. His love is focused on giving not only what we deserve, but what we do not deserve.

"Greater love hath no man than this, that a man lay down his life for his friends" (John chapter 15 and verse 13 (KJV). Only when we can realize the love our heavenly Father has for us can we love and live as families should live.

I want to take a moment to encourage men. Men, let's take the challenge to rise up and to take our rightful place, our God-given authority to lead our families by example because we are to be representatives of our heavenly Father in the way we live.

Godly men and women in Old Testament times knew that you cannot put a price on wholesome family values. I want to awaken you to the fact that the family is in trouble. I also want to help you to see that God is in control and He has the remedy to restore us as honorable and God-fearing families.

There is a battle going on to re-define the family and to re-define marriage. It is sad to hear things like "she has two mommies", or that "a marriage can be between two men." These days when we speak out against such things, we are threatened and accused of discrimination. By such things we can see just how far mankind has fallen and the degree of his depravity. But those of us who know the truth do not hate nor condemn them regardless to their lifestyle, but we pray that God will open their eyes to the truth that He calls such lifestyles sin. God wants us as Christians to show them by example how life should be lived as we commit our lives continually to Him. God established the family structure so that it would be a force of unity in the world; empowered by love with the aim of starting at home and spreading abroad. There is no force or power upon earth greater than the power of love. *"For God so loved the world, that He gave His only begotten son, that whosoever believeth in Him should not perish, but have everlasting life"* John chapter 3 and verse 16 (KJV).

The condition of families on earth in the last days is one of the chief signs that the end is near. God is gathering His children for that final day that the Bible calls "The day of the Lord" Malachi chapter 4 and verses 5-6 (KJV). The Lord is seeking to reunite families by restoring marriages, healing the wounded, and giving back what the enemy destroyed. Our hearts need to be open to the operation of God in this hour because He has brought us to a pivotal point in history, a time of change. The Spirit of God seems to be moving with urgency and with rapid response to this immediate need of renewal because His prize possession, the family, is in trouble. God always responds to the prayers of His people when we are faithful to live godly lives and are serious about serving Him.

The family has been under attack for a long time now and the enemy is not retreating. This is why families need to return to right standing with Almighty God. He is waiting patiently for us. If we expect to see a turnaround and recovery of the family to bring a positive impact on society and to re-establish God fearing communities, it must begin at home in our individual families.

The Old Testament prophet Elijah called the people of his day to repentance (1 Kings chapter 18 and verse 21). He called for them and urged them to make a definite commitment to Jehovah. The spirit of Elijah is still here today thanks to the Lord Jesus who compels us and requires a definite decision from us to repent. Parents should repent for sins against their children, and children should repent for sins against their parents, and let there be forgiveness among our people and within our homes. Repentance is a doctrine that has not gone out of style; it is still the way back to our heavenly Father. Read Jeremiah 6:16 for a more complete note on this. As a general rule, the more stable the parent the more stable the child. The more stable the home, the more stable the Church. Only through relentless love for God (stubborn faith), and the power of the Holy Spirit can godly men and women succeed in their plight to recover the family. To be restored, the family must maintain godly values, be in right standing before God, pursue Him with a passion, and pray to Him without ceasing. As we trust Him with unwavering faith, God will strengthen and vindicate the family; thus, restoring it to its rightful place once again.

I remember when I was growing up our family was very close. We were nowhere near being perfect, but we had lots of family time together. Prayer was a regular thing for my mother and Father in the home. It doesn't appear that families now days pray like they used to.

The family that the Lord wants is devoted to His cause. You know the saying: The family that prays together stays together? Well that saying is true. Even when they are grown up and if they have disagreements and are in separate corners of the world, the memories of childhood do not die; their spirit is still connected, and forgiveness is the way to re-unite. Families are broken up for so many different reasons that we cannot name them all; everything from I can't get along with him to; she said something that I didn't like.

Sometimes we can find ourselves trying to live life to please or to impress others; a thing that never is good.

Here is a true, wise and informative saying: If we live for other people's praises, we will die by their criticism. We have seen this play out on the world stage more so these days than ever before.

II Chronicles chapter 7 and verse 14 *says to us: If my people, which are called by my name, shall humble themselves and pray, and seek my face, and turn from their wicked ways: then will I hear from Heaven, and will forgive their sin, and will heal their land".*

Returning to wholesome family values will re-ignite revival that will spread like wildfire across the earth.

It's time for us to return to the Lord, because we are held accountable for the life we have been given.

When our lives are devoted to God's cause things will begin to change. Now we must learn to get beyond the traditional expression of devotion and learn to get into a Divine encounter. A Divine encounter will enable us to separate from the sins we have gotten so cozy with in our lives over the years. To have devotion is good, but maturity and honesty remind us everyday that our devotion alone will cater more to our emotions than anything else, which end up being nothing more than a religious ritual. The Bible spoke of a day when Jesus would deliver the family by reuniting it, or else the condition of it would end in a curse. In the book of Malachi Chapter 4 and verse 6, He says:

"And He shall turn the heart of the Fathers to the children, and the heart of the children to their Fathers lest I come and smite the earth with a curse".
He reunites the family, thus, escaping the curse.

The call is being made to us as individuals, as a family, as a city, as a state, as a Nation and to the whole world; let's turn back to the Lord so that our lives and the lives of future generations will enjoy the power of God's provision for humanity.

He is calling, who will answer the call so that He will bring restoration to our world?

The Greek word "Kairos" means: the appointed times of God. We are living in the Kairos of God's restoration campaign. So let's redeem the time; because it is short and so many are not saved.

If you love the Lord, you are part of His family, so rise up and take your proper place at the table He set for you. His feast is prepared for all the members of His family, but your seat has been vacant. He awaits your arrival.

Chapter 8

On Your Mark, Get Set, Live!

"Shall I bring to the birth, and not cause to bring forth, says the Lord; shall I cause to bring forth, and shut the womb says thy God?" Isaiah chapter 66 and verse 9.

The words of this scripture were given at a time of difficulty in the life of the Nation of Israel. But beyond their difficulties, God's focus was on bringing to pass the promises He had made to His chosen people. He would faithfully perform it.

In this chapter, I want to talk about the heritage and the inheritance that belongs to the believer.

Their meanings are basically the same.

Now, what do you think of when you hear the word heritage? A heritage consists of material things passed down from fathers to children. It's a legacy; which is: Any system that consists of certain values. As I stated in Chapter 4, our bodies consist of DNA which identifies us as unique individuals with Genes that have been passed down from our parents. Genes are "The reception of genetic qualities by transmission from parent to offspring" (Webster's Dictionary).

Our Heavenly Father has given His children an inheritance. For that reason, He tells us in the scriptures: *"Cast not away therefore your confidence, which hath great recompense of reward. For ye have need of patience, that, after ye have done the will of God, ye might receive the promise"* Hebrews chapter 10 and verse 35 (KJV).

In this verse the phrase "recompense of reward" (in Geek *"misthapodosia"*) means reward, something given for some service rendered. In the case of Christians, it is a life lived for Jesus. Jesus said, *"I am come that they might have life, and that they might have it more abundantly"* (John chapter 10 and verse 10). The abundant life is the inheritance given to the godly and, not to the ungodly. Although it is freely given to us, it will cost us a life of sacrifice to lay hold upon it and to maintain it. We must receive it by faith as God enables us to live it through His grace.

An inheritance is given upon conditions. This means that there are some requirements that are expected on the part of the offspring. Many people don't successfully obtain their heavenly inheritance simply because they expect everything to be easy. So they become discouraged when Satan comes and tries to make them miss out on it deceiving them, and attempting to keep them in the dark concerning it.

There are too many heritages lying desolate among people in the body of Christ. Do you feel like you are not making progress while in the process of obtaining your inheritance? Maybe it's time for you to do a self-examine by checking every area of your life. There may be inroads where Satan has been allowed access to block your progress. Some things that can hinder us from obtaining our spiritual heritage are; offense, no forgiveness, bitterness, procrastination, indecision, and the fear of change, just to name a few. You must deal with these immediately and aggressively if you expect to enjoy all that God has for you.

We have been given the authority to tell Satan *"That's enough! I'm taking my rightful place in the kingdom of God!"* We cannot afford to let the enemy bring discouragement or keep us from receiving what God has for us.

In obtaining our inheritance, we progress by a process. If you are hesitating to lay hold on your heritage because of some past failure in your life, God will meet you at the point of your failure and strengthen you from within by His power.

After Jesus arose from the dead, He sent His angel to meet the women at the tomb. He said to them "Tell my disciples, and Peter, I will meet them in Galilee." My point is this: Peter thought that Jesus would reject him because of his betrayal. But Jesus said, regardless of Peter's failures, tell him that I will meet him in the place where I promised that I would.

Forget the past. God has promised to meet you in the place where He said He would. Right there where your need is regardless of your past failures. It is time for you to get on with your life. When are you going to begin living that victorious, overcoming, and more than a conqueror life you have been called to in Christ? It's time to stop trying to live by your own strength and ability, you can't do it yourself. There is a time when we have to admit that we have been living according to our own understanding. Our strength has only been the arm of flesh. God has so much more for us than we could ever accomplish on our own in multiple lifetimes.

As a child is formed in the womb of its mother, so is the Church formed in the heart of Jesus Christ. We are formed into His likeness. The mother is the heartbeat (sustainer) of the child, just as Jesus Christ is to the Church. There are certain steps in pre-natal care that must be taken to ensure the proper development of the child. After the child has been delivered, the next few years are crucial to the proper development of the child. As children begin growing in life, they develop awareness of their surrounding. In the toddler stage of life, they depend more upon their parents as they mimic them. In order for us to grow into strong and mature people of God in spiritual things, we must mimic our Savior Jesus Christ.

When the family is on its way to the park or to some other family event, the children are not usually preoccupied with such things as how are we going to get there, or any other parental responsibilities. They leave all the grown-up stuff to their parents. They simply trust that dad and mom can handle whatever else is happening. So it must be with you and I concerning our heavenly father. Those who would walk the road of godly men and women learn the most valuable lessons of life, and the chief of these is trust. They know that they cannot slide by on partial dependence or partial trust; they must depend totally upon God and have complete trust in His wisdom and not theirs.

I believe the Lord has brought us to the place where we can now realize that He does not accept some of our ideas of who He is. He is holy, and He requires His children to be holy. He is not to become like us, but we are required to become like Him as the scriptures say: *"For as many as are led by the Spirit of God, they are the sons of God"* Romans chapter 8 and verse 14 (KJV).

Only the Holy Spirit can enable men to properly appropriate the principles of God's Kingdom on the earth. Living for Jesus is a privilege with great responsibility. It is the responsibility with the given authority of godly men and women to impact our society with the Gospel of Jesus Christ. And He has assured us of the following:

"What we bind on earth will be bound in heaven, and what we loose on earth will be loosed in Heaven" Matthew chapter 16 and verse 19 (KJV).

Satan, your enemy's time is limited. It is almost up. Although for a while he has freedom to operate in the earth realm, he cannot at all travel the corridors of Heaven. He has been cast out of and cut off from Heaven. Through godly living and the declaration of God's Word, we can bind Satan here on earth. When we as godly men and women are obedient to God's Word, the Holy Spirit enables us to put into effect the ordinances of Heaven in the earth, but we must be sure that what we say and do is according to God's Word.

With an enemy lurking around as a lion he is always ready to pounce. Sometimes he can make us feel like God is not working fast enough, and we want the Lord to hurry up. Then it is easy to misappropriate the principles of God's Word when we are impatient. When we attempt to help out the Lord, we end up trying to make the promises of God come to pass in our lives. We have to remember that this is not about us, it is about what God has ordained for our lives. It is about His plan of salvation that He established before the foundation of the world.

We must remember that His will is often realized through different seasons of life. I believe that one of our biggest hindrances to realizing God's best for us is that often we do not recognize the times and seasons that He has brought us into. Timing is everything, especially in God's program, He is precise, and His timing is accurate.

We may not always understand His ways, but still His ways are perfect, and we can be sure that *"He will work all things together for our good to them who love the Lord, to them who are called according to His purpose" Romans chapter 8 and verse 28* (KJV). Since this is our heritage given to us freely by the Lord, let us lay hold on it, it is ours to receive. Go for it!

Effective Shelf Ministry

There was a song written by a secular artist years ago titled, "It's my party and I'll cry if I want to." It sounded like a real sob story. It was more like a brat who just had to have it her way.

I find that things cannot be that way when one has made Jesus Lord of their life. When we accept His will for our lives, He leads the way for those He loves. In the course of their lives, He is working on something wonderful, I like to think: He brings us to greatness. Matthew chapter 3 and verse 11 tell us; *"But he that is greatest among you shall be your servant"*.

All the men and women of God from biblical times have set up the landmarks of Christendom, but they did not obtain this wealth of Christ's riches by their own merit. They were called by God, shaped into the image of His Son, and sent by Him. But what makes this so profound is that; as He sent them, He went with them and assured their victor, and over time He brought them to greatness.

We know them as heroes of the faith. Yes, heroes, however, before they could arrive at the place of greatness, God would order their steps, and through the power of His Holy Spirit they stepped sure-footed with vision to forge ahead. At times He moved them to work His will when they did not think it was time to move. At other times when they thought it was the right time for that dream to become a reality, or that promise to be fulfilled, He gave them a shelf Ministry. He put them on the shelf (a time of waiting). This was the time to develop that godly faith which had been bestowed upon them.

Where our faith is concerned, God must be in control if we are to affect any good changes in society. Everyone who chooses to live godly will experience what I call the Abraham experience. That is: a time of testing and waiting. In this time of testing and waiting God seeks to prove our sincerity and to determine if we will seriously take Him at His Word.

Too Good for the Shelf

After God has made a promise to us, then comes the testing of our faith. There are no great victories apart from having great faith. Now don't be afraid when you hear "Great faith". The definition of great faith is not necessarily a large amount of faith.

For example:

You are sure that God has called you to minister to others and He has given you a vision and a promise that He will do great things for you.

But now years have passed and you still have not seen the manifestation of it. Then you think: I could have done some great things for the Lord by now, … so now you think your faith is too small. Not so at all. But great faith simply means believing in a God who is great and who does great things.

The potency or impact of one's faith is not found in amounts, but in the three cords of trust, sincerity and consistency before the Lord. When our faith is grounded in these, we can expect to function effectively in ministry. God is preparing us and equipping us with this kind of faith when we have been placed on the shelf for a season.

The mentality of overnight success in ministry is the mindset of a person whose view has put a cloud over their faith. Ministry takes time to develop, as do those who will minister.

In ministry it is easy to want to acquire things in a hurry, but I caution you by the examples of countless others who have shown to us that when we acquire things in a hurry, we usually lose them in the same way.

So we learn what it means to be called into ministry in the times of waiting. While on this journey; as we learn to trust the Lord without growing impatient, we find the hidden nuggets of wisdom along the course. God knows that we grow impatient at times, and that it is so easy to lose sight on the bigger picture. The great truth of it all is that the Christian life is all about Jesus and not about us; this is where we re-focus and see the complete picture.

If God has put you on the shelf (a time of waiting), do not be alarmed about it, nor become impatient, just know that the Lord is not wasting time, but He is active on your behalf.

You are on the shelf for a time so that His purposes can be realized. The time is approaching for Him to bring you forth, but you must abide this time of preparation. When He is finished, your ministry will be more effective. So don't be in a hurry no matter how slow things may seem to be moving; God is still in control. If you think you are too good for what I call shelf ministry; which is patiently waiting for the Lord to move, then you will never realize your vision nor get God's best for you. It is always a good thing to remember, that no one, not even those who will become what we would classify as great because of their accomplishments; can ever be too good for the shelf. Ultimately, anyone who is willing to allow the Master's dealings with them to be complete position themselves for special use in His eyes. These Men and women have a shelf life that doesn't expire. This shelf life makes them and their Ministries prime candidates for greatness.

Job in his book asked this age-old question:

"If a man die, shall he live again? All the days of my appointed time will I wait, till my change come." Job chapter 14 and verse 14 (KJV).

In the King James Key Word Study Bible in verse 14, the word *again* is in italics. It indicates that the patriarch envisioned a resurrection of his body.

He uses phrases like, *"the grave"* and *"keep my secret"* (verse 13) even at a time when he had no written scripture to reference.

This reveals to us that he expected the resurrection of the body. His hope in God sustained (kept) him regardless to his infirmity. This means that although Job no doubt felt like he was dying, he knew that God was not yet finished with his life. The test he found himself in brought him face to face with the undeniable truth that his real life was not in his possessions or his notoriety, nor was his life to be found in all the good works he had done for others. Although these are admirable attributes of a Christian, he realized that real life is in God.

So we don't have to be shaken by the adversities of our times. We have a hope that reaches beyond the grave. We shall rejoice in Heaven someday, but Jesus promised us we would live in victory right here also while we are on the earth. Those who are more than conquerors know that life is found only in the Son.

"He that hath the Son hath life: And he that hath not the Son of God hath not life" 2 John chapter 5 and verse 12 (KJV).

This is the hour for the church to arise. Her task is to go on the offense and confront Satan on his own turf. No more must we stand in a position of being on the defense only, i.e., fighting Satan only when he attacks. In order to possess the blessings God has determined for us to enjoy, we must go on the offensive by declaring God's Word and acting on it; backed by a life of holiness. It is time to take a stand! Only then can we realize God's plan for our lives. Now is the time to take inventory of your life, to re-evaluate, re-calculate and re-direct your life by developing new habits that are built upon biblical principles.

Godly men of Old, who walked this path, have shown to succeeding generations that God is faithful in His call to men. Through their examples of obedience to Him, God's purpose for us is clearly seen so that we would set our hope in Him. Godly Men and Women of old did not let the conditions of life sway them from their God-given mission, nor did they let the distractions of the day take their eyes off their goal which was to please God. The key to their success was not in their own strength or wisdom, but in simple faith in God they moved mountains and turned the world upside down.

Conclusion

"Righteousness exalts a nation, but sin is a reproach to any people" Proverbs 14:34 (KJV).

Whether individually or collectively, on a national or global scene; the day that we learn to follow in the direction the Lord leads us, will be the day that we will experience drastic changes for good.

Although our world is filled with people whose lives are rooted in unrighteousness, God is still on His throne and in control of His creation.

He is preparing His troops in the earth for that great and final day when every man will give an account for the deeds done in the body. So this is the time and this is the hour that God has waited for to bless the body of Christ with unparalleled blessings, and unimaginable breakthroughs. The whole world will know of His saving grace and of His goodness.

Do not be alarmed by the tragic foreshadowing of end-time events. If you love the Lord, your reward awaits you.

"And, behold I come quickly; and my reward is with me, to give to every man according as his work shall be." Revelation chapter 22 and verse 12 (KJV). History has shown us that times of trouble never could, and never will, change God's mind about us. The first century church was born in the midst of persecution, but it did not stop true men of God from sharing the good news of His love. Regardless of all of Satan's attempts to discredit or cast doubts about Jesus' resurrection, consider what has been preserved and reserved for us through preceding generations.

If difficult times then were a vehicle for the gospel to travel upon in reaching what they knew then as the whole world, dare we think to fathom what God is able to do in our day upon which the end times have come? So it remains, as it is written in the holy scriptures *"Even from everlasting to everlasting thou art God"* Psalm chapter 90 and verse 2 (KJV).

God has plans for your life and where your steps should take you. At times that may call for us to step out into unfamiliar territory that brings us to places where our vulnerabilities are exposed. People may even ridicule us, yet we have examples; witnesses who have gone before us (read *Hebrews chapter 12 and verse 1*) whose voices collectively echo throughout history of God's Divine presence to heal and to deliver regardless of the odds.

I invite you to come and experience God's love and power to transform an ordinary person into an instrument for extraordinary Divine use. As we seize this opportunity to lay hold on eternal life, we will by the power of His divine strength come into the presence of the all-sufficient one who said:

"I am Alpha and Omega, the beginning and the end, the first and the last" Revelation chapter 22 and verse 13 (KJV). God is calling each of us to follow in the footsteps of the victorious one, Jesus the Christ of God; He who is one with God, walked with God.

About the Author

Willie Johnson was born July 23, 1952, in Laurinburg, North Carolina, to John and Lucy Johnson. He is the eighth of fifteen children. Willie received Jesus Christ as his Lord and Savior in the summer of 1972 after being strung out on drugs. After committing his life to Jesus, he became very active in the ministry. As a psalmist and lover of music, he played for various groups and choirs.

In 1986, he received the call of God and became active in the church as a deacon and trustee. In 1989, he was ordained as assistant pastor at the church where he worshiped, and after a few years, he became pastor. He served as pastor/senior pastor of two churches for more than six years in New Haven, Connecticut.

Currently, he is the President of King's Foundations Ministries, an outreach radio and media Ministry in Orlando Florida. He enjoys writing, playing and recording music, and singing for the Lord. He loves God for giving him this privilege to serve.